Adapting
Curricular
Materials

D0206558

Adapting Reading and Math Materials for the Inclusive Classroom

Jeanne Shay Schumm

Published by
The Council for Exceptional Children

A Product of the
ERIC/OSEP Special Project
The ERIC Clearinghouse on
Disabilities and Gifted Education

Library of Congress Cataloging-in-Publication Data

Schumm, Jeanne Shay, 1947–
    Adapting reading and math materials for the inclusive classroom :
kindergarten through grade five/ Jeanne Shay Schumm.
        p.   cm. — (Adapting curricular materials ; v. 2.)
    Includes bibliographical references.
    ISBN 0-86586-339-3
    1. Handicapped children—Education (Elementary)—United States.
2. Reading (Elementary)—United States.   3. Mathematics—Study and
teaching (Elementary)—United States.   4. Inclusive education—
United States.   I. Title.   II. Series.
LC4028.5.S35   1999
371.9′0444—dc21   99-12953
                                                                        CIP

ISBN 0-86586339-3

A product of the ERIC/OSEP Special Project, the ERIC Clearinghouse on
Disabilities and Gifted Education.

Published in 1999 by The Council for Exceptional Children, 1920 Association
Drive, Reston, Virginia 20191-1589

Stock No. P5306

This publication was prepared with funding from the U.S. Department of
Education, Office of Special Education Programs, contract no. ED-99-CO-0026.
Contractors undertaking such projects under government sponsorship are
encouraged to express freely their judgment in professional and technical
matters. Prior to publication the manuscript was submitted for critical review
and determination of professional competence. This publication has met such
standards. Points of view, however, do not necessarily represent the official
view or opinions of either The Council for Exceptional Children or the Department of Education.

Printed in the United States of America
10   9   8   7   6   5   4   3   2   1

Contents

Preface, v

Acknowledgments, xi

Introduction, 1

1. **Principles for Adapting Materials, 5**
   1. Feasible, 8
   2. Lively, 9
   3. Eliminated, 9
   4. EXplicit, 10
   5. Intentional, 11
   6. Beneficial, 12
   7. Limelight, 13
   8. Evaluated, 13
   References, 14

2. **Making Adaptations to Instructional Materials, 15**
   1. Providing Direct Assistance, 16

   Adaptation 1: ESP-Plus: Toward Constructive Collaboration in Making Curricular Adaptations, 17
      Developers: Jeanne Shay Schumm, Marie Tejero Hughes, Maria Elena Arguelles

   Adaptation 2: Enlisting and Empowering Other Adults: The Miami Reads Tutorial Project, 20
      Developers: Miami-Dade County Public Schools, Division of Language Arts and Reading, Norma Boussard (District Director), Alicia Moreyra (Project Leader)

Adaptation 3: Direct Assistance from Peers (An Example: Repeated Readings), 25

2. Structuring Lessons to Promote Learning from Materials, 30

   Adaptation 4: Planning Pyramid for Structuring Lessons for Diverse Learners, 30
   Developers: Jeanne Shay Schumm, Sharon Vaughn, Alexandra G. Leavell

   Adaptation 5: Planning Pyramid for Multilevel Word Recognition Instruction, 37

   Adaptation 6: Planning Pyramid for Multilevel Mathematics Instruction, 41

3. Simplifying or Supplementing Existing Materials, 44

   Adaptation 7: Story Reading Guides, 45
   Developers: Jeanne Shay Schumm, Marguerite Radencich Gerald E. Schumm

   Adaptation 8: Audiotaping, 50

4. Teaching Strategies for Using Materials, 53

   Adaptation 9: Collaborative Strategic Reading, 53
   Developers: Sharon Vaughn, Janette Kettman Klingner, Jeanne Shay Schumm

   Adaptation 10: SIR RIGHT: A Strategy for Math Problem Solving, 57
   Developer: Marguerite Radencich

A Final Word, 61

Preface

Teachers in inclusive classrooms regularly face the difficult task of having to modify the curriculum to reach all of their students, many of whom have special needs. Students with disabilities, whether physical, emotional, or cognitive in nature, respond to the curriculum differently from other students. For example, depending on the disability itself and other factors affecting their ability to succeed academically, students may need modifications such as advance and graphic organizers, instructional scaffolding, additional practice and time to complete assignments, and/or alternative media (e.g., large-print materials, audiotapes, or electronic materials). Without specific modifications, the standard curricular materials can be inadequate for these students, and too frequently they can find themselves blocked from access to essential aspects of the curriculum. Teachers must adjust the materials or their presentation to break down the barriers and assist these students in learning.

The IDEA Amendments of 1997 require that students with disabilities have access to the general education curriculum. This legislative requirement makes the accessibility of curricular materials an issue of even greater importance than it otherwise would be. To meet the goal of equal access to the curriculum for everyone, to enable each student to engage with his or her lessons in a meaningful way, teachers must be prepared to provide useful alternatives in terms of both curricular materials and instructional delivery. Well-adapted materials without an effective method of teaching are practically useless, but with the proper tools and instructional methods, a good teacher encourages each member of the class to participate directly in the learning experience.

Unfortunately, teachers who have to work with standard, off-the-shelf curricular materials usually have little time to develop accommodations for their classes. They need a guidebook that outlines successful adaptation strategies in clear, concise language, something that demonstrates the link between purpose and procedure for a teacher in a classroom of diverse learners. This ERIC/OSEP Mini-Library was designed to fill the gap for educators who are already engaged in curriculum adaptations as well as those who have not yet begun. The three volumes in this series

- Outline the conceptual strategies behind instructional adaptations.

- Present characteristics of classroom materials that allow for effective adaptations.

- Illustrate those adaptations in brief, process-oriented chapters and vignettes. The adaptations describe best or promising practices that are based upon relevant special education research.

The Mini-Library consists of three books:

1. An introductory overview on general principles of adaptation of curricular materials, written by Edward J. Kame'enui and Deborah Simmons of the University of Oregon.

2. A volume on adaptation for kindergarten through fifth grade, using the content areas of reading and math, by Jeanne Shay Schumm of the University of Miami.

3. A volume on adaptation in grades three through eight, in language arts, social studies, and science, by Jean Schumaker and Keith Lenz of the University of Kansas.

Clearly, three short volumes cannot cover the range of disabilities and other diverse learning needs that teachers have to confront. We have limited our consideration to mild cognitive disabilities and have focused on adapting materials rather than on delivery (although in practice the two go hand in hand). For those who wish to read more about adaptations, the books provide references to additional resources on effective teaching methods and research.

A Word on Universal Design

This Mini-Library proceeds from the assumption that teachers who have to adapt instruction for their students usually don't have a say in choosing the curriculum or designing the materials before they are expected to use them. This series of publications offers the means to facilitate that process. If the developers of curricular materials anticipated some of the needs that teachers face in inclusive classrooms, such as students who read below grade level or who have organizational or attention-deficit problems, and if they then designed accommodations for these needs into the materials, that would free up teachers to devote more time to teaching and less to adapting the curriculum. While this may sound like an ideal situation, actually it is neither unrealistic nor far in the future of public school classrooms. Over the past few years, there has been a concerted effort in special education to promote curricular materials with built-in adaptations, particularly in digital media, that are flexible and customizable. Known as *universal design for learning,* the movement is based on the principles behind the universal design movement for access to products and environments for all users, regardless of sensory or physical disabilities.

The educational strategies behind universal design for learning basically underlie any sort of classroom adaptations. When a teacher adapts a curriculum, she or he works to accommodate as many student needs as possible by developing an array of potential supports. An unadapted curriculum generally is one-size-fits-all, but adapted materials can be tailored to the students. In this way, universally designed materials can accommodate students where they need it, but those supports are incorporated during the development phase, rather than having to be added after the fact. The same strategies that teachers use to adapt inefficient or inconsiderate materials go into universally designed curricular materials. A history text, for example, is written to include graphic organizers and strategic questions to help students who would find a typical text inaccessible but also to provide a challenge for those who would otherwise find it boring or unengaging. A digital reading program can highlight the text word for word or sentence by sentence for students who have difficulty following along by themselves, or it can say the words out loud for those who need more familiarity with the sounds of what they read. Such adaptations could be designed and provided by teachers—and this Mini-Library provides a number of successful examples—but the more resources that come packaged with the curriculum, the greater its flexibility and the less it has to be modified by the teacher.

Although materials that incorporate aspects of universal design have yet to become routine in schools, school districts in several states already are using preadapted books and digital media in their classrooms. For example, under a Department of Education grant, the Center for Applied Special Technology (CAST) is currently working with the State of New Hampshire to study the potential of technology to promote literacy for all students. This project, now implemented in 16 New England schools, uses a CD-ROM-based instructional program, *WiggleWorks,* that employs principles of universal design for learning. Other states, such as Texas and California, are using such preadapted, technology-supported programs for curriculum delivery. As technology inevitably plays an increasingly central instructional role, the concept of universal design for learning will gain prominence.

A Final Word on Adaptations

No computer or other classroom tool, no adapted materials can ever take the place of the teacher. Without an informed and dedicated teacher directing the learning, without someone who knows the students well enough to know what barriers to break down and where and how much to challenge a student, then even the best tools will be useless. Universally designed and adapted curricular materials are intended to provide teachers with more time and better means to get the job done, not to do the job for them.

Acknowledgments

Many people contribute their invaluable time and skills to a project such as this, and they need to be acknowledged. This Mini-Library resulted from a need to update a popular publication on curricular adaptations developed 10 years ago by the ERIC/OSEP Special Project. In late 1997, the Special Project, under the aegis of and with the support of the Office of Special Education Projects (OSEP), convened a group of researchers and practitioners to discuss the best ways to address the need for adapted materials in the inclusive classroom. Those intensive discussions and subsequent suggestions resulted in the outline for this series of books. We extend our appreciation to the researchers and teachers involved in the initial stages of this project and to authors Kame'enui, Lenz, Schumaker, Schumm, and Simmons, who agreed to devote a large portion of their time to this project in addition to their regular duties. We hope this Mini-Library will be a valuable tool for both special and general educators.

The manuscripts were graciously and carefully reviewed by a number of practitioners and researchers in the field. Their comments helped us to help the authors tighten the expression of their ideas. Special thanks are extended to Louise Appel, Pamela Burrish, Russell Gersten, Kathy Haagenson, Pauletta King, John Lloyd, Patricia Mathes, and Elba Reyes.

Special appreciation goes to Lou Danielson, director of OSEP's Research to Practice Division, whose commitment to these activities is borne out by his participation at each stage of development. The staff of the ERIC/OSEP Special Project at The Council for Exceptional Children were responsible for the meeting described previously and for conceptualizing and editing the three volumes. They are Kathleen McLane, Ray Orkwis, and Jane Burnette. All of us involved in developing these materials hope you will find them useful in your work, and we welcome your responses.

Nancy Safer
Executive Director
The Council for Exceptional Children

Acknowledgments

My deepest thanks to The Council for Exceptional Children for the invitation to compile adaptations for the elementary volume of the Mini-Library. This exercise has offered me the opportunity to reflect on the past 10 years of my professional life and to recognize how fortunate I have been to collaborate with some of the best professionals in the field. There are so many people to thank.

First, Marguerite Radencich. Margie and I were doctoral students together at the University of Miami. We wrote our first books and articles together. She went on to become a national leader in the field of reading and was appointed coeditor of *The Reading Teacher*. Her untimely death occurred during the writing of this manuscript. What I remember most about Margie is her enormous capacity for work—always centered on making the world of learning better for students and teachers. Thanks, Margie.

Second, Sharon Vaughn. I had the opportunity to work along with Sharon and numerous colleagues in our Office of School-Based Research (both on campus at the University of Miami and as colleagues in the schools) on many of the adaptations included in this volume. Being a part of that research team was one of the most exhilarating professional experiences of my life, perhaps because we conducted research with a heart—always with the dream of helping all students learn and helping teachers access the tools to make it happen. Sharon Vaughn, now at the University of Texas at Austin, was and is a catalyst for both the head and the heart. Thank you, Sharon, for a fabulous ride!

Third, the Miami Reads Tutorial Program team. Norma Boussard and Alicia Moreyra of the Miami-Dade County Public Schools and Josh Young of Miami-Dade Community College are the spark plugs igniting a collaborative effort for tutoring students in our schools and after-school programs. They have provided so much energy in bringing together school and community resources. Thank you for inviting me to be part of your team.

Fourth, Zhigang Zhang and Kerri Schaffer. Zhang, a recent graduate of our doctoral program, and Kerri, a student in our master's program, provided expert assistance in the preparation of this volume. Thank you for your energy and time.

Fifth, Ray Orkwis. Ray, the editor of the Mini-Library series, has provided me with support and encouragement throughout the drafting and editing of this book. Thank you for your expertise and for your interest in bringing concrete suggestions to teachers.

Finally, Jerry, Jamie, and John. Thank you, family, for being with me every step of the way.

Introduction

The majority of students with mild disabilities receive some, if not all, of their education with their general education peers. This has become increasingly more common in recent years with the movement toward full-time inclusion of students with disabilities in general education classrooms (Lewin, 1997; National Joint Committee on Learning Disabilities, 1993). In addition, recent surges in immigration have led to increased cultural and linguistic diversity in classrooms in the United States. Because of these changes in the demographic composition of classrooms, the notion of "one-size-fits-all" instruction is no longer a viable approach. For a variety of reasons, many students cannot keep pace with the curriculum as it is structured for the mainstream. Ironically, even though more students are included in general education classrooms they may still feel excluded from the basic right to learn.

In-class segregation can be diminished, if not eliminated, with the use of well-planned, skillfully implemented instructional adaptations. *Adaptations* are adjustments that teachers make to provide students with the systems and support they need to be successful learners. These adaptations might be routine or incidental, short-term or long-term, individualized or not. Adaptations might be actual changes to the materials students use or to the instructional practices related to those materials. The good news is that students of all grade groupings and achievement levels appreciate teachers who make adaptations (Schumm & Vaughn, 1994; Vaughn, Schumm, Niarhos, & Daugherty, 1993; Vaughn, Schumm, Niarhos, & Gordon, 1993). The bad news is that students (and their parents) often do not feel that they are getting the adaptations they need (Schumm, Vaughn, & Saumell, 1992).

Classroom teachers shoulder the primary responsibility for meeting the educational needs of all students in the classroom, in spite of the fact that many teachers have not learned how to accommodate students with academic, cultural, or linguistic differences in their preservice or inservice professional development programs (Schumm & Vaughn, 1992). Moreover, many teachers have not had the opportunity to develop expertise in working with a wide array of other professionals (e.g., Title 1 teachers, special education teachers) with whom they may now coteach (Bauwens & Hourcade, 1995; Cook & Friend, 1995; Reinhiller, 1996). Teachers who are familiar with instructional accommodations frequently indicate that adaptations are desirable in promoting student learning, but they are not always logistically possible to implement due to barriers such as class size and lack of adequate instructional resources (Schumm & Vaughn, 1991). Consequently, even experienced, competent, caring teachers cannot always provide students with challenges in learning to read, write, and compute with the accommodations they need (Schumm, Vaughn, Haager, McDowell, Rothlein, & Saumell, 1995).

Purpose and Focus of the Book

The primary purpose of this book is to provide elementary school teachers (grades K–5) with suggestions and guidelines for making adaptations for students with mild disabilities in the general education classroom. We focus on reading and mathematics because difficulty in mastering these tools for learning is the primary reason for referral for special education services in the elementary grades. Providing youngsters the instruction they need in learning to read and compute and to apply those competencies in real-world applications is a fundamental goal of elementary education. When children do not meet this fundamental goal, it is of dire concern to parents and teachers alike.

This book is not intended to be comprehensive in scope. Rather, it is intended as a handbook, providing basic tools for organizing classrooms for adaptations, and as a sampler of adaptations that have been used successfully in elementary classrooms. Teachers, as well as administrators, are encouraged to view the book as a springboard for thinking flexibly and creatively about how to meet the challenge of teaching a wide range of students in the classroom. With flexibility and creativity on the part of a team of caring, competent professionals, this challenge can be met! If there is a true team effort in the school, teachers and administrators will work together and administrators can encourage teachers to consider and apply adaptations in their classes.

How the Book Is Organized

The book is organized into two chapters. Chapter 1 presents eight principles for materials adaptation organized according to the acronym FLEXIBLE. Chapter 2 provides suggestions for making adaptations to materials for reading and mathematics instruction in the elementary grades. The suggestions are divided into four categories: providing direct assistance, structuring lessons to promote learning from materials, simplifying or supplementing existing materials, and teaching strategies for using materials.

Authors' note: Much of the research on which the text of this introduction is based was conducted at the University of Miami Office of School-based Research under the direction of Sharon Vaughn and Jeanne Shay Schumm. The first-person references relate to this research group rather than the general editorial "we."

References

Bauwens, J., & Hourcade, J. J. (1995). *Cooperative teaching: Rebuilding the schoolhouse for all students.* Austin, TX: Pro-Ed.

Cook, L., & Friend, M. (1995). Co-teaching: Guidelines for creating effective practices. *Focus on Exceptional Children, 29,* 1–16.

Lewin, T. (1997, December 28). Where all doors are open for disabled students. *The New York Times,* pp. 1, 12–13.

National Joint Committee on Learning Disabilities. (1993). Providing appropriate education for students with learning disabilities in regular education classrooms. *Journal of Learning Disabilities, 26,* 330–332.

Reinhiller, N. (1996). Co-teaching: New variations on a not-so-new practice. *Teacher Education and Special Education, 19,* 34–48.

Schumm, J. S., & Vaughn, S. (1991). Making adaptations for mainstreamed students: General classroom teachers' perspectives. *Remedial and Special Education, 12,* 18–27.

Schumm, J. S., & Vaughn, S. (1992). Planning for mainstreamed special education students: Perceptions of general classroom teachers. *Exceptionality, 3,* 81–98.

Schumm, J. S., & Vaughn, S. (1994). Students' thinking about teachers' practices. *Advances in Learning and Behavioral Disabilities, 8,* 105–129.

Schumm, J. S., Vaughn, S., Haager, D., McDowell, J., Rothlein, L., & Saumell, L. (1995). General education teacher planning: What can students with learning disabilities expect? *Exceptional Children, 61,* 335–352.

Schumm, J. S., Vaughn, S., & Saumell, L. (1992). What teachers do when the textbook is tough: Students speak out. *Journal of Reading Behavior, 24,* 481–503.

Vaughn, S., Schumm, J. S., Niarhos, F., & Daugherty, T. (1993). What do students think when teachers make adaptations? *Teaching and Teacher Education, 9,* 107–118.

Vaughn, S., Schumm, J. S., Niarhos, F., & Gordon, J. (1993). Students' perceptions of two hypothetical teachers' instructional adaptations for low achievers. *Elementary School Journal, 94,* 87–102.

1
Principles for Adapting Materials

Access to the mainstream reading and mathematics curriculum is not about place (Vaughn & Schumm, 1996). Simply placing students with mild disabilities in the general education classroom and issuing them a grade-level textbook is not enough. Appropriate and reasonable adaptations are needed if the individual student's basic right to learn is to be ensured. But how can this be accomplished? How can the busy professional implement adaptations for individual children while maintaining the equilibrium of the class as a whole? The answer is flexibility.

In this chapter you'll learn about eight principles for making adaptations in the elementary classroom. Our conversations with teachers have helped us learn that the task of meeting individual needs is not always easy, but with some flexible, creative thinking it can be done. These principles are derived from years of research in general education classrooms that include students with disabilities (for summaries, see Schumm & Vaughn, 1994; Schumm & Vaughn, 1995). Surveys, individual interviews, and focus group interviews with students and teachers, as well as classroom observations, have provided important information about what is needed for student success, what adaptations students and teachers prefer, and what is reasonable for general education teachers to implement. Teachers are encouraged to keep these principles in mind when selecting adaptations to meet the needs of individual students.

The principles have been organized using the acronym FLEXIBLE. Each principle is accompanied by a set of questions that teachers can use in selecting potential adaptations (see Figure 1). The eight principles can be triggered using the key words described here.

The "FLEXIBLE" Acronym
Feasible
Lively
Eliminated
EXplicit
Intentional
Beneficial
Limelight
Evaluated

FIGURE 1
The FLEXIBLE Principle:
Questions to Ask Before Selecting Potential Adaptations

1. *Feasible:* Successful adaptations must be feasible for classroom teachers to implement.

   • When can I fit the adaptation into the daily schedule?
   • What human and/or material resources do I have to implement the adaptation?
   • What human and/or material resources do I need to implement the adaptation?

2. *Lively:* Successful adaptations must be lively, engaging, and/or fun.

   • How can I use the adaptation to promote active learning?
   • How can I plan this adaptation to be interesting and fun?
   • What strategies can I use to motivate the student(s) so that I can continue to use this adaptation over a period of time?

3. *Eliminated:* Successful adaptations must be developed with the goal of working toward independence with a gradual fading and eventual elimination of the adaptation.

   • What steps are needed to fade the adaptation over a period of time?
   • What additional instruction do I need to provide to work toward the eventual elimination of the adaptation?
   • How will the student use this adaptation as a step to another skill or as a regular part of his or her repertoire?

4. *EXplicit:* Successful adaptations must have a definite purpose—a purpose that is made

   • What is the intent or purpose of this adaptation?
   • How will I communicate the purpose of the adaptation to the student?

continues

6

FIGURE 1 *(Continued)*

explicit to students, other professionals in the classroom, parents, and, if necessary, the student's peers?

- What other people need to know about the adaptation (e.g., parents, other professionals, other students)?
- How will I communicate the purpose of the adaptation to others?

5. *Intentional:* Successful adaptations should be part of a comprehensive plan for the student with disabilities.

- How does this adaptation fit with goals on the student's IEP?
- How does this adaptation fit with goals and objectives set by district and/or state guidelines?

6. *Beneficial:* Successful adaptations should benefit the student with disabilities and either enhance or at least not detract from the learning of other students in the classroom.

- How does the adaptation benefit the student with disabilities?
- Can other students benefit from the adaptation as well?
- How can I implement the adaptation so that it enhances and does not detract from the learning of other students in the classroom?

7. *Limelight:* Successful adaptations do not place undue attention on the student with disabilities or put the student in a potentially embarrassing situation.

- How and when can I implement the adaptation so that it does not put the student with disabilities in an unfavorable position?

8. *Evaluated:* Successful adaptations are evaluated on an ongoing basis.

- How effective is the adaptation in promoting learning for the student?
- What impact does the adaptation have on the social adjustment of the student?
- What does the student like and dislike about the adaptation?
- What do the parents like and dislike about the adaptation?
- What do I need to change about the adaptation?
- Is the student ready to take on a higher level of independence?

1. Feasible

Successful adaptations must be feasible for classroom teachers to implement.

The first principle of making adaptations is that adaptations must be feasible to use. While teachers may recognize the desirability of an adaptation in terms of promoting student learning, if the adaptation is not "doable," it is less likely to be implemented on an ongoing basis. For example, rewriting mathematics word problems using more readable terminology and bullets to highlight key steps may be desirable in helping a student read and understand, but the feasibility of the teacher's being able to rewrite the text week in and week out is not very high.

Addressing the feasibility of adaptations is in no way meant to imply that teachers are lazy or are not interested in meeting the needs of students. It is a pragmatic reality—limited planning time, instructional time, and resources, coupled with overcrowded classes, make it a practical necessity to think of efficient and effective ways to teach all students.

Some adaptations are naturally more feasible to implement than others (Schumm & Vaughn, 1991). Adaptations such as establishing appropriate routines, providing reinforcement and encouragement, and establishing reasonable expectations are relatively easy to accomplish. Others, such as rewriting regular materials, using alternative materials, and individualizing instruction, require some consideration of logistics. In the case of adaptations that are more logistically complicated, feasibility can be enhanced through the imaginative use of additional resources, both human (e.g., volunteers, parents, paraprofessionals, other students) and material (e.g., technology, supplemental materials, manipulatives).

In evaluating potential adaptations for feasibility, the key questions are as follows:

- When can I fit the adaptation into the daily schedule?
- What human and/or material resources do I have to implement the adaptation?
- What human and/or material resources do I need to implement the adaptation?

2. Lively

Successful adaptations must be lively, engaging, and/or fun.

The more lively, engaging, and fun the adaptation, the more likely it is that students will like it and will tolerate its continued use. One common criticism of remedial teaching practices is that they are dull, repetitive, and uninviting and cause students to become disengaged and discouraged. The same holds true for adaptations for students with disabilities in the general education classroom.

In selecting adaptations, the "customer satisfaction" element should be considered using the following questions:

- How can I use the adaptation to promote active learning?

- How can I plan this adaptation to be interesting and fun?

- What strategies can I use to motivate the student(s) so that I can continue to use this adaptation over a period of time?

3. Eliminated

Successful adaptations must be developed with the goal of working toward independence, with a gradual fading and eventual elimination of the adaptation.

Ideally, an adaptation should serve as a temporary scaffold to support student learning.[1] If the scaffold is not gradually removed, the student does not have the opportunity to work toward independence. One reading specialist recently voiced complaints during individualized education program (IEP) meetings about the use of audiotaped textbooks as an instructional adaptation. Her concern was that audiotapes

---

[1]For a further discussion of the principle of scaffolding, see Volume 1 of this series, pp. 17–20.

were being used as a substitute for teaching children how to read.[2] Adaptations should be thought of as a temporary support—a support that will eventually be faded and eliminated with supplemental instruction.

Here are some questions to guide thinking about the elimination issue:

- What steps are needed to fade the adaptation over a period of time?

- What additional instruction do I need to provide to work toward the eventual elimination of the adaptation?

- How will the student use this adaptation as a step to another skill or as a regular part of his or her repertoire?

4. EXplicit

Successful adaptations must have a definite purpose—a purpose that is made explicit to students, other professionals in the classroom, parents, and, if necessary, the student's peers.

Adaptations are most effective when they are purposeful. If students understand how the adaptation will help them learn and are aware of the potential benefits, it is more likely to be well received and sustained. The purpose also should be made clear to other professionals working in the classroom and to parents. The more key stakeholders who are informed and supportive of the additional help, the better.

Explaining an adaptation to a student's peers can be a sticky matter. At the elementary school level, adaptations can be implemented without taunting and discord if the teacher sets a positive classroom climate in which individual differences are tolerated and even appreciated. There are times when some students think that getting extra help, extra time to take a test, or less difficult homework is simply not fair. In

---

[2] The use of audiotapes as an unmediated adaptation must be approached with great caution. For a fuller discussion of a successful adaptation using audiotapes, see Volume 3 of this Mini-Library, pp. 34–36. Also, when the goal is not to teach reading but to enhance content area comprehension, audiotaping can be a successful strategy; see Adaptation 8 of this volume (pp. 50–53) for an appropriate use of audiotaping of text.

such cases, a simple, direct explanation may be needed. For the most part, students are tolerant of adaptations and appreciate teachers who take the time to implement them.

Following are questions to consider related to issues of explicitness:

- What is the intent or purpose of this adaptation?
- How will I communicate the purpose of the adaptation to the student?
- What other people need to know about the adaptation (e.g., parents, other professionals, other students)?
- How will I communicate the purpose of the adaptation to others?

5. Intentional

Successful adaptations should be part of a comprehensive plan for the student with disabilities.

Classroom observations reveal that general education teachers do make some adaptations for students with mild disabilities (McIntosh, Vaughn, Schumm, Haager, & Lee, 1993; Schumm et al., 1995). Most frequently, adaptations are made during a lesson when a student doesn't seem to be grasping a concept or mastering a skill. However, such adaptations tend to be idiosyncratic, incidental, and not part of a comprehensive plan for the student. While some on-the-spot adaptations are warranted, successful adaptations should be used routinely and be part of a larger plan to help students grow toward independence. Adaptations should also be planned in light of the goals set in the student's IEP. A makeshift adaptation may be "overkill" or inadequate when considered in this longer-range context. Also, an adaptation should consider the goals set by the state or district, as well as the assessment process for students with disabilities.

In thinking about an adaptation, teachers should consider the following questions:

- How does this adaptation fit with goals on the student's IEP?
- How does this adaptation fit with goals and objectives set by district and/or state guidelines?

6. Beneficial

Successful adaptations should benefit the student with disabilities and enhance, or at least not detract from, the learning of other students in the classroom.

An adaptation should provide an educational benefit for the student with disabilities. However, some adaptations can be considered to be just good teaching techniques and can be used with all students in the classroom. For example, study guides to help students read difficult informational material can benefit students at all achievement levels (Schumm, Vaughn, & Saumell, 1992).

When considering the selection of an adaptation the teacher should also bear in mind the needs of students with language differences. If teachers have to make separate adaptations for students with disabilities and separate adaptations for students with language differences, the temptation is not to make adaptations at all. Students with disabilities and those with language differences have unique learning needs, and teachers should not lump those differential needs into one package. However, many adaptations, such as graphic organizers, are recommended for both groups of students. To the degree that it is possible, teachers should implement adaptations that meet a wide array of student needs.

Finally, a common issue confronting teachers is the "Robin Hood" effect (Slavin, Karweit, & Madden, 1989). Some parents, teachers, administrators, and even students are concerned that adaptations require stealing time and resources from the "rich" (higher-achieving students) to give to the "poor" (lower-achieving students). The author observed a higher-achieving fourth grader who spent most of her school day tutoring a student with learning disabilities. While student pairing is an excellent instructional adaptation, in this case it was overused, to the detriment of both students.

In selecting and implementing adaptations, the following questions can help teachers think about potential benefits:

- How does the adaptation benefit the student with disabilities?

- Can other students benefit from the adaptation as well?

- How can I implement the adaptation so that it enhances and does not detract from the learning of other students in the classroom?

7. Limelight

Successful adaptations do not place undue attention on the student with disabilities or put the student in a potentially embarrassing situation.

Recently a parent of a child with learning disabilities told the author, "My daughter refuses to have any individualized adaptations. She doesn't want to appear different from other students. She'd rather do it herself and fail than be in the spotlight." Parents, teachers, and students echo this theme. As much as possible, the adaptation should be a normal part of the classroom activities. Thus, it is important to think of the following question when planning for implementation of an adaptation:

- How and when can I implement the adaptation so that it does not put the student with disabilities in an unfavorable position?

8. Evaluated

Successful adaptations are evaluated on an ongoing basis.

Once an adaptation is implemented, it needs to be evaluated periodically. The teacher should evaluate the adaptation to see whether desired results are being obtained. If not, adjustments and alternatives need to be considered. If so, fading or perhaps eliminating the adaptation may be appropriate.

The evaluation should also engage parents, students, and, when possible, administration and support personnel in the process. In some districts, support team and IEP meetings include the parents, teacher, resource teacher, administrator, school psychologist, speech pathologist, and others. During parent conferences the adaptation can be explained and reviewed to obtain parental input about the academic and social impact of the adaptation. Even very young students have definite opinions about what helps them learn and what does not. From time to time student evaluations of an adaptation can be conducted to find out what students think.

Questions to guide thinking about evaluation of adaptations are as follows:

- How effective is the adaptation in promoting learning for the student?

- What impact does the adaptation have on the social adjustment of the student?

- What does the student like and dislike about the adaptation?

- What do the parents like and dislike about the adaptation?

- What do I need to change about the adaptation?

- Is the student ready to take on a higher level of independence?

References

McIntosh, R., Vaughn, S., Schumm, J. S., Haager, D., & Lee, O. (1994). Observations of students with learning disabilities in general education classrooms. *Exceptional Children, 60,* 249–261.

Schumm, J. S., & Vaughn, S. (1991). Making adaptations for mainstreamed students: General classroom teachers' perspectives. *Remedial and Special Education, 12,* 18–27.

Schumm, J. S., & Vaughn, S. (1994). Students' thinking about teachers' practices. *Advances in Learning and Behavioral Disabilities, 8,* 105–129.

Schumm, J. S., & Vaughn, S. (1995). Getting ready for inclusion: Is the stage set? *Learning Disabilities Research and Practices, 10,* 169–179.

Schumm, J. S., Vaughn, S., Haager, D., McDowell, J., Rothlein, L., & Saumell, L. (1995). General education teacher planning: What can students with learning disabilities expect? *Exceptional Children, 61,* 335–352.

Schumm, J. S., Vaughn, S., & Saumell, L. (1992). What teachers do when the textbook is tough: Students speak out. *Journal of Reading Behavior, 24,* 481–503.

Slavin, R. E., Karweit, N. L., & Madden, N. A. (1989). *Effective programs for students at risk.* Boston: Allyn & Bacon.

Vaughn, S., & Schumm, J. S. (1996). Classroom ecologies: Classroom interactions and implications for inclusion of students with learning disabilities. In D. S. Speece & B. K. Keogh (Eds.), *Research on classroom ecologies: Implications for inclusion of children with learning disabilities* (pp. 107–124). Hillsdale, NJ: Erlbaum.

2
Making Adaptations
to Instructional Materials

The eight principles of adaptation selection (FLEXIBLE) can be useful in the selection and evaluation of an individual adaptation. This chapter provides not only specific examples of adaptations of instructional materials, but also frameworks for planning and organizing for adaptations. Why? Over the years elementary general and special education teachers have told researchers that they know how to make adaptations. Their challenge is to know how to plan and organize the school day and available personnel to make it all happen. For consistency, the 10 suggestions in this section are labeled *adaptations* even though some of the suggestions are planning or organizational frameworks rather than specific adaptations.

Adaptation of materials for students at the elementary level can take many forms and can vary in terms of the amount of teacher involvement (in planning, preparation, and instruction), student independence, and requirements for additional resources. In planning for support for an individual child or group of children, teachers can consider adaptations from the following categories (Schumm & Strickler, 1990):[3]

1. Providing direct assistance.

2. Structuring lessons to promote learning from materials.

---

[3]Schumm, J. S., & Strickler, K. (1990). Guidelines for adapting content area textbooks: Keeping teachers and students content. *Intervention in School and Clinic, 27*, 79–84.

---

3. Simplifying and supplementing existing materials.

4. Teaching strategies for students to use materials.

1. Providing Direct Assistance

Perhaps the most demanding adaptations in terms of time and resources are those requiring direct interaction of the student with another human being. From the perspective of teachers, parents, and students, one-to-one assistance in learning from instructional materials from a trained professional is the ideal for students with extraordinary educational needs. Direct assistance in learning from instructional materials can take many forms:

- Reading printed materials aloud to the student.

- Providing guided instruction before, during, and after reading printed materials.

- Adjusting the pace of instruction.

- Teaching prerequisite information so that students can use materials independently.

- Monitoring student understanding and mastery in the use of materials.

- Reteaching if necessary.

However, providing such assistance is not an economic reality in most general education settings or, increasingly, in special education settings where the student caseload is unusually high. How else can teachers ensure that students have the intensity of instruction and support they need to be successful with the curricular materials? Teachers who are the most successful in providing direct assistance are those who use constructive collaboration with other professionals and enlistment and empowerment of other adults and who promote positive peer instruction among students.

Suggested adaptations for providing direct assistance include the following:

- ESP-Plus: Toward Constructive Collaboration in Making Curricular Adaptations

- Enlisting and Empowering Other Adults: The Miami Reads Tutorial Project
- Direct Assistance from Peers (An Example—Repeated Readings)

Adaptation 1: ESP-Plus:
Toward Constructive Collaboration
in Making Curricular Adaptations

One way to increase the amount of direct assistance available to elementary school students is through coteaching. Due to the inclusion movement and the reduction of Title 1 pullout programs, more and more classrooms have two or more professional teachers for all or part of the school day. While coteaching holds the promise of more and better adaptations for students with special needs, many general and special education teachers have neither the professional training nor the experience to work in such partnerships.

Two teachers with whom the author worked explained to her early in the school year: "We make a perfect pair. I know what (she) is thinking before she says a word. We have ESP." Despite this optimistic attitude, as the school year progressed their partnership unraveled, for a variety of reasons. Since that time, conversations with over 200 general and special education teachers involved in coteaching partnerships have taught us that intuition and assumption are insufficient for successful coteaching to occur. Successful coteaching requires more than extrasensory perception (ESP). Careful planning of roles and responsibilities is imperative. This includes consideration of what adaptations need to be made and who will prepare for and actually make those adaptations.

What is the adaptation?

ESP-Plus is a series of recommendations for successful coteaching partnerships (Schumm, Hughes, & Arguelles, 1998). Successful coteaching partnerships enable both professionals to maximize their potential as educators and to provide all students with the direct assistance they need. The recommendations are derived from a variety of data sources (i.e., individual interviews, focus group interviews, and open-ended survey items) included in a statewide pilot program focusing on general–special education partnerships (see Arguelles, Schumm, & Vaughn, 1996, for a technical report).

Overall, teachers reported positive perceptions of coteaching—not only in terms of personal job satisfaction, but also in terms of the impact on general education and special education students. However, teachers did offer recommendations for improving the coteaching experience. Their comments have been organized around the abbreviation *ESP*.

E = Engagement, Expectations, Elasticity

- *Engagement.* Both teachers need to be actively engaged in teaching using a variety of grouping patterns (Vaughn, Schumm, & Arguelles, 1997) and techniques for monitoring student understanding (Schumm, Vaughn, & Sobol, 1997).

- *Expectations.* General and special educators may have very different views of what to expect from students. Issues related to student expectations—especially as they pertain to grading and pacing of instruction—need to be discussed and negotiated.

- *Elasticity.* Working collaboratively necessitates flexibility. It is a primary ingredient for coteaching success.

S = Skills, Support, Structure

- *Skills.* Recognizing the skills of each professional and developing mutual skills (particularly communication and interpersonal skills) can enhance the working relationship.

- *Support.* Administrative support is especially important for the coteaching partnership to succeed.

- *Structure.* Classroom management (structure) issues can be more troublesome than philosophical issues related to curriculum. Constant communication about management issues needs to occur.

P = Planning, Preparation, Parity

- *Planning.* Collaborative planning time is a must. Without time to make short- and long-range plans, the coteaching partnership cannot exist.

- *Preparation.* Ongoing professional development is needed as teachers continue to prepare for new teaching situations.

- *Parity.* If coteaching is to succeed, the basic premise must be that there are two professionals in the classroom.

What does it look like in practice?

Sandra Alexander (special education teacher) and Bart Miller (general education teacher) coteach in a fourth grade classroom that includes seven children with learning disabilities. Sandra teaches in three classrooms. Because all seven students have reading-related learning disabilities, she is with Bart during reading and content area (science/social studies) periods of the day.

At the beginning of the school year, Sandra and Bart set aside one full day for initial conversations and joint planning. They used the ESP-Plus framework to discuss basic issues related to coteaching. Several important issues emerged. Bart had never taught in an inclusive classroom before, so he admitted that he had much to learn about what to expect academically and socially from the students with disabilities. Sandra admitted that science and social studies content was not her strength, but that she did have a great deal to share in terms of strategy instruction and possible adaptations. They decided that they wanted to communicate to parents and students that they were a team. Consequently, a desk was set up for Sandra to use while she was in the room, and all correspondence related to reading and content area instruction was sent to parents with both teachers' names.

A major part of their discussion revolved around roles and responsibilities for making adaptations to instructional materials. Their goal was to provide all students with the direct assistance they need to succeed. During the reading period, Sandra planned to pull a small group of students for intensive word recognition instruction. She also agreed to construct weekly story reading guides to help students with reading problems participate in whole-class discussions of basal reader stories and trade books.

For science and social studies, Bart volunteered to write study guides for each unit if Sandra would provide insights for students with special needs during their planning time. Sandra said she would enlist volunteers from the fifth grade class to audiotape science and social studies chapters for students with reading difficulties to listen to at home. Both agreed to commit to weekly planning sessions to coordinate their activities, and both agreed to be actively involved during lessons to monitor student understanding and to make on-the-spot adaptations as needed.

Sandra describes her partnership with Bart this way:

It works because we work at it. We started off with communication, and even though there's not a great deal of time for coplanning, it's our top priority. It's important for the students that we have our act together. When we understand our roles and responsibilities, so do the students. We actually write down who is going to do what. It's a living document that changes from time to time, but we have found it helpful to put our responsibilities on paper. The students know that help is available from one or both of us. Moreover, since we divide the preparation tasks for materials adaptations, we get the job done. We have a rhythm now; we feel it and so do the students.

Having two professionals in the classroom offers the promise of providing students direct assistance in learning from instructional materials. However, it takes more than ESP to make it happen. It takes engagement, expectations, elasticity, skills, support, structure, planning, preparation, and parity. It takes a new kind of professional collaboration between general and special educators—a collaboration that can only result in positive student academic and social outcomes.

What additional information is available?

Schumm, J. S., Hughes, M. T., & Arguelles, M. E. (1998). *Co-Teaching: It takes more than ESP.* Unpublished manuscript. To obtain manuscript, e-mail Jeanne Schumm (schumm@miami.edu).

References

Arguelles, M. E., Schumm, J. S., & Vaughn, S. (1996). Executive Summaries for ESE/FEFP Pilot Program. Report submitted to the Florida Department of Education.

Schumm, J. S., Vaughn, S., & Sobol, M. C. (1997). Are they "Getting It?" How to monitor student understanding in inclusive classrooms. *Intervention in School and Clinic, 32,* 168–171.

Vaughn, S., Schumm, J. S., & Arguelles, M. E. (1997). The ABCDEs of co-teaching. *TEACHING Exceptional Children, 30*(2), 4–10.

Adaptation 2: Enlisting and Empowering Other Adults: The Miami Reads Tutorial Project

Classroom teachers—particularly at the elementary school level—state that their knowledge, skills, and confidence in making adaptations for students with special learning needs is moderate to high (Schumm & Vaughn, 1992). The greater problem for teachers is how and when to find the time in the busy school day—in sometimes overcrowded classes—to make those adaptations.

Increasingly, teachers are being encouraged to engage other adults in supportive teaching roles in the classroom (Schumm & Schumm, 1999; Wasik, 1998). The other adults might be parents, community volunteers, service learning students from high schools and universities, paid tutors, or other paraprofessionals. Adults who are empowered with adequate training, are monitored and supported in their work, and have well-defined instructional roles and responsibilities can provide students with direct assistance.

What is the adaptation?

Early prevention of reading failure has been a major concern of educators and policymakers in recent years. Obviously, if systematic, intensive reading instruction is provided in the early years, the need for special education and other remedial services in subsequent years of schooling can be diminished. Unfortunately, many early intervention programs are cost prohibitive in that they require one-to-one instruction, special curricular materials, and/or highly trained personnel.

In 1997, President Clinton launched the America Reads challenge. The charge was to engage volunteers and paid tutors in a sweeping initiative focused on early intervention to prevent reading failure, with the idea that all students in the United States would learn to read by third grade. Part of this initiative was the funding of college work-study students to serve as paid tutors in schools and social service agencies. The challenge was how to recruit, train, monitor, and evaluate literally thousands of well-intentioned but largely inexperienced tutors.

Miami-Dade County Public Schools responded to this challenge with a collaborative effort between the school district and local institutions of higher education (i.e., Barry University, Florida International University, Florida Memorial College, Miami-Dade Community College, University of Miami). School district personnel spent a summer adapting and then field testing materials initially developed as part of the Book Buddies program implemented in Charlottesville, Virginia (Invernizzi, Juel, & Rosemary, 1997; Juel, 1991). Adaptations included procedures for tutoring students who are English-language learners, refinement of recordkeeping procedures, and refinement of assessment tools. The target student audience was first grade students. Instructional routines were developed to focus on rereading of familiar materials, sight words, phonological awareness and letter recognition, and reading–writing connections. The result was an instructional manual, instructional materials, and training procedures for tutors, classroom teachers, school reading specialists, and administrators. That same summer an advisory committee consisting of school district personnel, university personnel, and representatives from the community at large met to discuss logistical components of the program (e.g., recruitment and training of tutors, monitoring tutors in the field, liability issues, parent communication, program evaluation).

During the 1997–1998 school year the program was started in 34 elementary schools and 8 community service agencies in the Miami-Dade County area. Approximately 300 tutors worked with over 1,500 elementary school students during one-on-one tutoring sessions. The Miami Reads Tutorial Project is exemplary not only in terms of what a large, urban public school district can accomplish, but also in terms of procedures that individual classroom teachers can use to engage and empower other adults in providing direct assistance to students. Following are 10 key components that contributed to the success of the program:

1. Clear, systematic instructional procedures.

2. Curricular content and literature that are consistent with regular classroom instruction.

3. Active learning that promotes student engagement.

4. Adequate training for tutors.

5. Adequate training for school-based personnel—both administrative and instructional.

6. Designation of a school-based leader who can handle interviewing, monitoring, scheduling, and evaluating tutors.

7. Assessment materials that clearly define a student's academic needs and can track student achievement over a period of time.

8. A record-keeping system that is simple and direct, yet provides a log of each tutoring session and a student's accomplishments during the session.

9. Instructional materials that are inexpensive and readily available.

10. A system for familiarizing and possibly involving parents with the program.

Because of the program's success, program planners have initiated efforts to expand it. Parents and school volunteers are being trained as tutors, Volunteers in Service to America (VISTA) volunteers have been brought on to supervise tutors in the field, and a tutoring plan for intermediate readers is now in the development process.

As Topping (1998) cautioned, tutors are not teachers. Tutors need adequate training, careful monitoring, and carefully structured materials. According to Topping, "tutoring should be complementary rather than supplementary; it should never substitute for professional teaching" (p. 48). Nevertheless, programs such as Miami Reads Tutorial Project hold promise for direct assistance for students who would not normally have that opportunity.

What does it look like in practice?

Olga Rodriguez teaches first grade in a Miami-Dade County Public School. She has 34 students in her class. During the 1997–1998 school year, Ms. Rodriguez's school participated in the Miami Reads Tutorial Project. At the beginning of the school year Ms. Rodriguez and the reading specialist in her school attended a full-day professional development workshop related to Miami Reads. During that time they learned about the content of the program, assessment procedures, scheduling tutoring sessions, the roles and responsibilities of all key stakeholders (i.e., administrators, reading specialists, teachers, tutors, parents), and how to interpret the program to parents.

During the weeks following the training, Ms. Rodriguez worked with the reading specialists in her school to administer pretests of phonological awareness and letter recognition to her students. She identified five students who she felt most needed one-to-one tutoring. Each of the five students was tutored three times a week in half-hour sessions by one of two tutors (college students) assigned to her classroom. Ms. Rodriguez later requested that her part-time paraprofessional also be trained in the tutoring procedures to fill in on the days college tutors had exams or other commitments. All tutoring occurred during the school day in a small room adjacent to the media center. Ms. Rodriguez spent about 1 hour each week reviewing records from tutoring sessions, making necessary adjustments in instructional plans, and preparing reading materials for each of her students. During each session tutors followed the instructional routine outlined in the materials and amended by Ms. Rodriguez.

Ms. Rodriguez evaluated the program as follows:

> The thing about the Miami Reads Program that I like best is that it is consistent with my instructional program. The tutor follows the same scope and sequence that I do in teaching sight words and phonological awareness skills. The tutor is also able to do repeated readings of predictable books that I introduce to all students in my class. Without the extra help my five stu-

dents get, they would be sure to fall through the cracks. They need the extra practice that I just don't have time to give. The recordkeeping system is great—I can see just how students are getting along.

An evaluation of the Miami Reads Tutorial Project was conducted to document the program (Schumm, Moreyra, & Young, 1999). Data sources included student academic data as well as instruments designed to elicit perceptions of the program from key stakeholders: administrators, reading coordinators and classroom teachers, tutors, and students (primarily first graders). Student academic measures of reading and spelling indicated that students made progress in letter recognition, letter production, phonemic awareness, and story reading. Moreover, tutors and school-based personnel provided testimony (through focus group interviews and surveys) to the overall progress of students who participated in the program. Evaluation of the program is ongoing. Students who participated in year one of the program are being followed to track their progress in grades two and three. Data also are being collected for students engaged in the second year of the program.

Who can provide additional information?

Miami-Dade County Public Schools
Division of Language Arts and Reading
1400 Biscayne Boulevard
Miami, FL 33132
305/995-1949

What additional information is available?

Pinnell, G. S., & Fountas, I. C. (1997). *Helping America read: A handbook for volunteers.* Portsmouth, NH: Heinemann.

References

Invernizzi, M., Juel, C., & Rosemary, C. A. (1997). A community volunteer tutorial that works. *The Reading Teacher, 50,* 304–311.

Juel, C. (1991). Cross-age tutoring between student athletes and at-risk children. *The Reading Teacher, 45,*178–186.

Schumm, J. S., Moreyra, A., & Young, J. (1999). *Miami Reads Tutorial Project: A community-based tutorial program.* Manuscript in preparation.

Schumm, J. S., & Schumm, G. E. (1999). *The reading tutors handbook: A commonsense guide to helping students read and write.* Minneapolis, MN: Free Spirit.

Schumm, J. S., & Vaughn, S., (1992). Planning for mainstreamed special education students: Perceptions of general classroom teachers. *Exceptionality, 3*, 81–98.

Topping, K. (1998). Effective tutoring in America Reads: A reply to Wasik. *The Reading Teacher, 52*, 42–50.

Wasik, B. A. (1998). Using volunteers as reading tutors: Guidelines for successful practices. *The Reading Teacher 51*, 562–569.

Adaptation 3: Direct Assistance from Peers (An Example: Repeated Readings)

When asked about reasonable adaptations teachers can make to support learning from instructional materials, some of the most frequently cited adaptations are those involving peer support (i.e., cooperative learning groups, student pairing) (Schumm & Vaughn, 1991; Schumm, Vaughn, & Saumell, 1994). Fortunately, students like working in small groups and in pairs (Elbaum, Schumm, & Vaughn, 1997) and appreciate it when teachers provide structure in teaching students how to work together and learn from each other (Elbaum, Moody, & Schumm, in press).

What is the adaptation?

Nonfluent readers typically read in a piece-by-piece, word-by-word manner and are slower and less accurate than fluent readers in decoding. With such inadequate reading patterns, nonfluent readers typically fall behind their peers and do not find enjoyment in reading. Moreover, because their reading is laborious, understanding of text is hampered.

The method of repeated reading was developed to help nonfluent readers improve fluency and, ultimately, reading comprehension. Initially, repeated reading for students with reading and learning disabilities was designed as a one-to-one clinical intervention (Heckelman, 1969; Samuels, 1979). This is not always possible for teachers to schedule in the busy school day. How can teachers provide students with the direct assistance they need to become more fluent readers? Teachers can incorporate repeated reading in the weekly routine using one or more grouping patterns so that peers can provide each other with direct assistance and support.

How to Teach It

Start by working with students to develop a purpose for repeated reading. This can be done through a brainstorming session initiated with the question "What are some things we learn that are improved with practice?" Explain to your students that reading needs practice, too, and best of all, reading practice can be fun!

Next, model repeated reading using the following procedure:

1. Select a book you will enjoy reading to your students again and again.

2. Read the story aloud as if you were a child reading it for the first time.

3. Include behaviors that might characterize a first reading, such as stopping to focus on difficult words.

4. After reading, talk about some parts that were difficult for you, and reread sentences to improve your reading.

5. Read the story a second time. During this reading, improve fluency, reduce the number of miscues, and add greater intonation and expressiveness.

6. With successive readings, become more expressive, fluid, and animated to achieve greater fluency and to promote greater comprehension and enjoyment.

Repeated Reading in Groups

Repeated reading can be incorporated in whole-class or small-group instructional routines. Big Books (i.e., books with large pictures and words that can be seen by the whole group), posters, or overhead transparencies are ideal for repeated readings in groups. Pointers can be used to keep students on track.

Repeated Reading in Pairs

Students can be grouped in pairs to read to each other. This pairing can be either informal or formal. The pairing can be with same-age or cross-age peers (Bergeron, 1998).

Koskinen and Blum (1985) discussed a procedure for informal repeated readings in pairs. With the informal pairing, each child selects his or her own passage to read to a partner. The first reader reads the self-selected passage three times. After the second and third reading, the first reader tells the partner how his or her reading improved and notes this improvement in a reading log. The listener provides support with new words as needed. Then the students switch roles and repeat the process. The activity takes 10 to 15 minutes.

Classwide Peer Tutoring (CWPT) is a more formal, structured way to provide students with paired practice (Delquadri, Greenwood, Whorton, Carta, & Hall, 1986; Mathes, Fuchs, Fuchs, Henley, & Sanders, 1994). CWPT differs from the informal procedure just described in that teachers appoint pairs (usually one more proficient reader with one less proficient reader), select reading material (at the lower reader's independent level), and allow the readers to read the same material to each other. The more proficient reader goes first, reading aloud to the partner for 5 minutes. The less proficient reader reads next, reading the same passage as the first reader. During CWPT sessions, which last approximately 30 minutes, students complete the repeated reading routine and also engage in correction, summarization, and prediction exercises. Students work with a carefully developed "script" that helps them to follow the sequence of activities and to provide feedback in sensitive and productive ways. As students work through the script they can earn points as a pair. Intensive instruction is necessary to prepare students, but once the procedures are understood, they become automatic.

Repeated Reading Individually

While direct assistance from peers is worthwhile and productive, it does have its limitations. Some students need more interactions with a trained professional to make progress in reading. There are several ways teachers can structure practice for students who need more intensive help in becoming more fluent readers. One way is through the use of a tape recorder. The student can practice reading into a tape recorder. When he or she is finished practicing and self-monitoring using a tape recorder, then the student can read to the teacher. Of course, individual practice with repeated readings can be facilitated by engaging the help of classroom volunteers and parents. Teachers can plan for regular monitoring of individual students' repeated readings by having "students of the day." For example, the teacher might have three "Monday" children who read to him or her during a center time. Other children are assigned on other days of the week. This rotation provides a systematic way to plan for monitoring of student repeated readings.

What research backs it up?

Numerous research studies have documented the impact of repeated reading in improving reading fluency and word recognition accuracy and in playing a significant role in improving reading comprehension (e.g., O'Shea, Sindelar, & O'Shea, 1987; Rashotte & Torgesen, 1985).

Repeated reading is a key component in such instructional practices as Classwide Peer Tutoring. A substantial body of research underscores the potency of Classwide Peer Tutoring (e.g., Delquadri et al., 1986; Mathes et al., 1994). Moreover, Classwide Peer Tutoring is an instructional practice that elementary school teachers and students seem to like (Vaughn, Hughes, Schumm, & Klingner, 1998).

What does it look like in practice?

Ms. Yaden has planned a variety of repeated reading activities for her second grade class. Each week she selects one trade book or poem related to her current thematic unit for a whole-class repeated reading. She selects books or poetry with predictable rhymes or story patterns. Classwide Peer Tutoring is part of the regular schedule on Mondays, Wednesdays, and Fridays. The activity takes only 20 minutes or so, but Ms. Yaden has seen that her students have made progress in becoming more fluent readers in a short period of time. From time to time she takes a break from more structured Classwide Peer Tutoring and lets children select their own reading material and their own partners during the paired reading period.

Four of Ms. Yaden's students need even more practice with repeated readings and even more careful monitoring. She has trained her paraprofessional in how to conduct repeated readings on a one-to-one basis. Ms. Yaden has planned for daily practice sessions for each child with the paraprofessional. Ms. Yaden has also scheduled a rotation so that she can listen to each of the children at least once a week and record their progress in their reading portfolios.

What additional information is available?

Fuchs, D., Mathes, P. G., & Fuchs, L. S. (1993). *Peabody Classwide PeerTutoring reading methods* (Unpublished teacher's manual). (Available from Douglas Fuchs, P.O. Box 328, George Peabody College, Vanderbilt University, Nashville, TN 37203).

Mathes, P. G., Fuchs, D., & Fuchs, L. S. (1995). Accommodating diversity through Peabody Classwide Peer Tutoring. *Intervention in School and Clinic, 31,* 46–50.

O'Shea, L. J., & O'Shea, D. J. (1988). Repeated reading. *TEACHING Exceptional Children, 20*(2), 26–29.

References

Bergeron, J. (1998). *A comparison of classwide cross-age and same-age peer tutoring for second-grade students at risk for reading failure.* Unpublished doctoral dissertation, University of Miami, Coral Gables, FL.

Delquadri, J., Greenwood, C. R., Whorton, D., Carta, J. J., & Hall, R. V. (1986). Classwide peer tutoring. *Exceptional Children, 52,* 535–542.

Elbaum, B., Moody, S. W., & Schumm, J. S. (in press). Mixed ability grouping for reading: What students think. *Learning Disabilities Research and Practice.*

Elbaum, B., Schumm, J. S., & Vaughn, S. (1997). Urban middle-elementary students' perceptions of grouping formats for reading instruction. *Elementary School Journal, 97,* 475–500.

Heckelman, R. G. (1969). A neurological impress of remedial reading instruction. *Academic Therapy Quarterly, 4,* 277–282.

Koskinen, P. S., & Blum, I. H. (1985). Paired repeated reading: A classroom strategy for developing fluent reading. *The Reading Teacher, 40,* 70–75.

Mathes, P. G., Fuchs, D., Fuchs, L. S., Henley, A. M., & Sanders, A. (1994). Increasing strategic reading practice with Peabody Classwide Peer Tutoring. *Learning Disabilities Research and Practice, 9,* 4–48.

O'Shea, L. J., Sindelar, P. T., & O'Shea, D. J. (1987). The effects of repeated readings and attentional cues on the reading fluency and comprehension of learning disabled readers. *Learning Disabilities Research and Practice, 20,* 103–109.

Rashotte, C. A., & Torgesen, J. K. (1985). Repeated reading and reading fluency in learning disabled children. *Reading Research Quarterly, 20,* 180–188.

Samuels, S. J. (1979). The method of repeated readings. *The Reading Teacher, 32,* 403–408.

Schumm, J. S., & Vaughn, S. (1991). Making adaptations for mainstreamed students: General classroom teachers' perceptions. *Remedial and Special Education, 12,* 18–27.

Schumm, J. S., Vaughn, S., & Saumell, L. (1994). Assisting students with difficult textbooks: Teacher perceptions and practices. *Reading Research and Instruction, 34,* 39–56.

Vaughn, S., Hughes, M., Schumm, J. S., & Klingner, J. K. (1998). A collaborative effort to enhance reading and writing instruction in the inclusion classroom. *Learning Disabilities Quarterly, 21,* 57–74.

Author's note: Thanks to Suzette Ahwee for her expert assistance in earlier drafts of this adaptation.

2. Structuring Lessons to Promote Learning from Materials

Many adaptations are made on the spot during regular classroom instruction. While a teacher is teaching a lesson, he or she may observe that one or more students aren't getting it or may need additional support to learn a concept or skill or to complete a task. Indeed, most of the adaptations classroom teachers make are incidental and in response to immediate student needs.

While incidental modifications may be necessary and appropriate, it is also imperative for teachers to be intentional in making adaptations. Successful adaptations should be part of a comprehensive plan for students with mild disabilities. As teachers get to know their students, some student needs can be anticipated and appropriate adaptations planned for before the lesson begins. The Planning Pyramid (Figure 2) is a tool to help teachers plan for adaptations for diverse learners. Although the Pyramid initially was designed for planning for content area lessons, teachers can also use it to plan for multilevel lessons in reading and mathematics.

Suggested adaptations for structuring lessons to promote learning from materials include the following:

- Planning Pyramid for structuring lessons for diverse classrooms.

- Planning Pyramid for multilevel word recognition instruction.

- Planning Pyramid for multilevel mathematics instruction.

Adaptation 4: Planning Pyramid for Structuring Lessons for Diverse Learners

Elementary classes in the United States are becoming increasingly more diverse in terms of their linguistic, cultural, and academic composition. This diversity becomes particularly challenging when teachers plan for reading assignments. Although textbooks in all content areas remain the primary tool teachers have for planning instruction, the reality is that many textbooks are simply too difficult for students who lack the decoding skills, vocabulary, and prior knowledge necessary to read and comprehend demanding text material.

Three broad dilemmas face elementary school teachers as they plan reading assignments in any subject area. First, textbooks are frequently difficult in terms of readability level for at least some students in the classroom. Second, textbooks characteristically are dense in

FIGURE 2
Basic Components of the Planning Pyramid

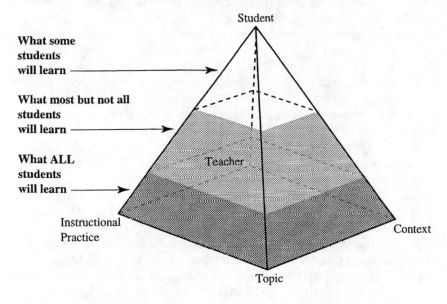

What some students will learn

What most but not all students will learn

What ALL students will learn

Student

Teacher

Instructional Practice

Context

Topic

Note. From Schumm, J. S., Vaughn, S., & Leavell, A. G. (1994, May). Planning Pyramid: A framework for planning for diverse students' needs during content area instruction. *The Reading Teacher, 47,* 608–615. Nancy Padak and Timothy Rasinski, Eds. Copyright by International Reading Association.

respect to the number of new concepts teachers must introduce within a relatively short period of time. Third, many teacher's editions of textbooks do not offer specific suggestions for helping teachers meet the diverse needs of a variety of learners in their classrooms (Schumm, Vaughn, Haager, & Klingner, 1994). Consequently, teachers often are left on their own in thinking about how best to help all students learn.

While textbook adaptations and other effective instructional methods for helping students cope with difficult text are readily available to most teachers, the gulf between preferred practice and prevailing practice still exists (Wood & Muth, 1991). Why? Research on teachers' perceptions of textbook adaptations provides some clues (Schumm, Vaughn, & Saumell, 1994). Elementary school teachers report that they feel they have the knowledge and skills to make textbook adaptations and that they generally are willing to make adaptations, but that they sometimes do not make them because they are too time consuming or difficult to implement when planning for the class as a whole.

What is the adaptation?

To assist teachers in planning for textbook adaptations, Schumm, Vaughn, and Leavell (1994) worked collaboratively with classroom teachers to develop a framework for planning for diverse student needs, the Planning Pyramid. The Pyramid is based on the idea that all students can learn, but not all students learn at the same pace. It is a tool for planning for differentiated instruction in general education classrooms.

The Planning Pyramid is composed of five points of entry and three degrees of learning (see Figure 2). There are five points, or axes, of the Pyramid, which represent the factors teachers consider when planning any lesson: (1) the topic, (2) the students, (3) the classroom context, (4) the teacher, and (5) appropriate instructional practices. The questions in Figure 3 are typical reflections teachers make when planning a lesson. The points of entry are interrelated and interdependent and have a strong impact on lesson planning.

Using the insights gained from teacher reflection about the points of entry, the next step is to determine what will be taught and how. The degrees of learning help teachers think through the content of a lesson (i.e., concepts or skills to be learned) and think about appropriate instructional practices to help all students learn. The teacher first identifies these key concepts or skills and then categorizes the content in terms of three degrees of learning: (1) what all students will learn (base of the Pyramid), (2) what most, but not all, students will learn (middle of the Pyramid), and (3) what some students will learn (top of the Pyramid). Next, the teacher identifies instructional practices and adaptations. More intensive adaptations are necessary for the base of the Pyramid—material that *all* students in the classroom should learn.

Teachers who work with the Pyramid have told us that it is important not to lock students into Pyramid levels. Depending on a student's interest and prior knowledge of a topic, he or she may go right to the top at times. Also, students with special needs may go to the top if appropriate accommodations are provided. All students should have access to all information. In no way should the Pyramid be thought of as a way to track students or limit expectations.

Some teachers prefer to use the Planning Pyramid for individual lessons, others for weekly or unit plans. Either way, teachers who have used the Pyramid have taught us that clear identification of content expectations helps them to communicate more clearly with students, with parents, and with other professionals in the classroom.

To summarize, the Planning Pyramid is an effective planning tool for structuring instruction in diverse classrooms. The intent of the Planning Pyramid is to provide a framework for including all students

FIGURE 3
Questions for Reflective Planning
for Diverse Student Needs

Questions pertaining to the topic:

☐ Is the material new or review?
☐ What prior knowledge do students have of this topic?
☐ How interesting is the topic to individual students?
☐ How many new concepts are introduced?
☐ How complex are the new concepts?
☐ How clearly are concepts presented in the textbook?
☐ How can I relate this material to previous instruction?
☐ When considering all topics I am responsible for covering this school year, how important is this topic in the overall curriculum?

Questions pertaining to the teacher:

☐ Have I taught this material before?
☐ What prior knowledge do I have of this topic?
☐ How interesting is the topic to me?
☐ How much time do I have to plan for the unit and individual lessons?
☐ What resources do I have available to me for this unit?

Questions pertaining to students:

☐ Will a language difference make comprehension of a particular concept difficult for a student?
☐ Will students with reading difficulties be able to function independently in learning the concepts from text?
☐ Will a student with behavior or attention problems be able to concentrate on this material?
☐ Will there be students with high interest or prior knowledge of these concepts who would be anxious to explore the topic in greater breadth or depth or share their knowledge with classmates?
☐ Will my students have the vocabulary they need to understand the concepts to be taught?
☐ What experiences have my students had that will relate to this concept? Is there some way to relate this concept to the cultural and linguistic backgrounds of my students?

continues

FIGURE 3 *(Continued)*

Questions pertaining to context:

☐ Are there any holidays or special events that are likely to distract students or alter instructional time?
☐ How will the class size affect my teaching of this concept?
☐ How well do my students work in small groups or pairs?
☐ Which students need to work together?
☐ What access to materials do I have to teach this topic?

Questions pertaining to instructional strategies:

☐ What methods will I use to motivate students and to set a purpose for learning?
☐ What grouping pattern is most appropriate?
☐ What instructional strategies can I implement to promote learning for all students?
☐ What instructional adaptations can I implement to assist individuals or subgroups of students?
☐ What learning strategies do my students know or need to learn that will help them master these concepts?
☐ What in-class and homework assignments are appropriate for this lesson?
☐ Do some assignments need to be adapted for children with disabilities?
☐ How will I monitor student learning on an ongoing, informal basis?
☐ How will I assess student learning at the end of the lesson?
☐ How will I assess student learning of lesson material at the end of the unit?

Note. From Schumm, J. S., Vaughn, S., & Leavell, A. G. (1994, May). Planning Pyramid: A framework for planning for diverse students' needs during content area instruction. *The Reading Teacher, 47,* 608–615. Nancy Padak and Timothy Rasinski, Eds. Copyright by International Reading Association.

in the classroom as promising, successful learners who are full participants in the classroom learning community.

What research backs it up?

The Planning Pyramid was evaluated with elementary school teachers who participated in a 14-week research project. The purpose of the research was to determine feasible ways to help teachers plan for differential student needs. Participants were required to plan their lessons for science and social studies using their assigned textbooks and the Planning Pyramid. The qualitative study incorporated multiple data sources, including individual and focus group interviews, written lesson plans, and videotaped teaching episodes.

What does it look like in practice?

Ms. Martinez used the Planning Pyramid to design a nutrition lesson for her third grade students. Ms. Martinez has 32 students in her classroom, many of whom speak a language other than English in their homes. Three students with learning disabilities (reading at approximately a first grade level) are included in her classroom during science and social studies.

Ms. Martinez used school district curricular objectives and her assigned textbook to identify key concepts to be learned during the lesson. She also realized that the nutrition unit was one repeated in subsequent grades as part of a spiral curriculum, so her students were likely to encounter many of the concepts again. Fortunately, the nutrition lesson was one that could build on students' prior knowledge of and interest in food.

The Planning Pyramid for the nutrition lesson is included in Figure 4. Ms. Martinez first identified the key concepts that all, most, and some students would learn. She then identified instructional strategies for all students and adaptations for students with special learning needs. It was important to Ms. Martinez that all students had access to all information and that each of the students in her class had an opportunity to be a full participant in the lesson. She realized that some of her students would not master all of the information, but she also knew that her students would encounter the information again in upper grades or through television/public service programs.

Ms. Martinez monitored student understanding using individual K-W-L charts (Ogle, 1986). At the beginning of the lesson she determined what students already knew (K) about food labels and what they wanted to learn (W) by having them record this information on an individual chart. At the end of the lesson students recorded what they learned (L). For students with severe writing challenges, a teacher's aide recorded their dictated responses. Observation of responses during a sorting activity was a second way Ms. Martinez could monitor student understanding. Overall, Ms. Martinez was pleased with student outcomes. She noted that some reteaching was necessary (particularly in sorting foods by high and low fat, carbohydrate, protein) and planned a follow-up center activity for students who needed additional practice to master the objective.

FIGURE 4
Nutrition Lesson Plan

Date: 10/9 _____ Class Period: _Content_ _____ Unit: _Nutrition_ _____
Lesson Objective(s): _Introduce students to food labels_ _____
_____
_____

Materials	Evaluation
Food containers: cans, boxes, bags Reading passage from text	Individual K-W-L charts

In-Class Assignments	Homework Assignments
Sorting activity	Find five food labels at home; bring to class for group activity on Monday

LESSON PLANNING FORM

Pyramid	Agenda
What some students will learn: • How and when food labels changed in recent years • Other components of food labels	1) Whole class K-W-L activity. What I know about food labels; What I want to learn about food labels.
What most students will learn: • How to interpret total fat, total carbohydrate, total protein on labels • Food & Drug Administration (FDA) controls information on labels	2) Cooperative learning activity, read passage about food labels; Complete food sorting activity.
What ALL students should learn: • U.S. government requires food labels • Locate labels on food products • Sort foods by high and low fat, carbohydrate, protein	3) Complete K-W-L chart. What I learned about food labels.

Note. From Schumm, J. S., Vaughn, S., & Harris, J. (1997, July/August). Pyramid power for collaborative planning. *TEACHING Exceptional Children, 29*(6), 62–66. Copyright by The Council for Exceptional Children.

What additional information is available?

Schumm, J. S., Vaughn, S., & Harris, J. (1997). Pyramid power for collaborative planning. *TEACHING Exceptional Children, 29*(6), 62–66.

Vaughn, S., Bos, C. S., & Schumm, J. S. (1999). *Teaching exceptional, diverse, and at-risk students in the general education classroom* (2nd ed.). Boston: Allyn & Bacon.

References

Ogle, D. (1986). KWL: A teaching model that develops active reading of expository text. *The Reading Teacher, 39,* 564–570.

Schumm, J. S., Vaughn, S., Haager, D., & Klingner, J. K. (1994). Literacy instruction for mainstreamed students: What suggestions are provided in basal reading series? *Remedial and Special Education, 15,* 14–20.

Schumm, J. S., Vaughn, S., & Leavell, A. (1994). Planning Pyramid: A framework for planning for diverse student needs during content area instruction. *The Reading Teacher, 47,* 608–615.

Schumm, J. S., Vaughn, S., & Saumell, L. (1994). Assisting students with difficult textbooks: Teacher perceptions and practice. *Reading Research and Instruction, 34,* 39–56.

Wood, K. D., & Muth, K. D. (1991). The case for improved instruction in the middle grades. *Journal of Reading, 35,* 84–91.

Adaptation 5: Planning Pyramid for Multilevel Word Recognition Instruction

The topic of how best to teach word recognition to elementary school children has provoked heated debate for decades. This controversy has escalated in recent years, with researchers, educators, parents, and the community at large becoming engaged in the debate (Adams & Bruck, 1995). The challenge of optimal word recognition for students representing a variety of reading levels is particularly acute in highly diverse classrooms that include students for whom learning to read is very difficult (Schumm et al., 1995).

One approach to providing appropriate instruction for all students is through the use of multilevel instructional practices (Hall & Cunningham, 1996; Vaughn, Hughes, Schumm, & Klingner, 1998). Multilevel instructional practices are designed to provide for the needs of students with a wide range of reading levels and to incorporate adaptations for materials as needed. While a variety of grouping arrangements may be used to provide multilevel instruction (whole class, small group, pairing), the composition of the groups is generally heterogeneous. The basic premise of multilevel instruction is that all students have an opportunity to "plug in" to appropriate instruction and to receive support from teachers and from peers.

What is the adaptation?

The Planning Pyramid can be used to structure lessons for multilevel word recognition instruction. Although the Planning Pyramid was designed originally for content area reading instruction, after working with thousands of teachers in scores of college-level classes and professional development workshops, we have broadened the scope of the Planning Pyramid. Teachers have demonstrated that the Pyramid is also a viable planning tool for multilevel skills instruction.

In thinking about using the Planning Pyramid for word recognition instruction, the following questions need to be considered:

1. What is the word recognition competency to be taught?

2. What are prerequisites for this competency?

3. What does it take for students to master the competency (e.g., adaptations, extra repetition, support from an adult or peer)?

4. What are extensions and applications of the competency?

One multilevel instructional practice that is particularly amenable to the Planning Pyramid is *Making Words* (Cunningham & Hall, 1994a, 1994b). *Making Words* (and its intermediate grade extension, *Making Big Words*) is a word recognition/spelling activity that is designed for whole-class instruction. The *Making Words* activity is based on word families and leads students through a series of word-building and word-sorting activities. Students like *Making Words* because it is fast paced and involves the use of manipulatives (individual letters to make words).

What does it look like in practice?

Ms. Wagner uses the Planning Pyramid to structure her *Making Words* lessons on a weekly basis (see sample in Figure 5). The series of weekly lessons contains some review word patterns and a new target pattern that all students should learn. Ms. Wagner frequently needs to provide additional practice sessions with a few students with more acute

FIGURE 5
Weekly *Making Words* Lesson Plan

WEEKLY LESSON FORM

Week of: 3/9   Grade Teacher: Wagner (2) Subject: Lang. Arts

Objectives: Review -ar; -at patterns; Introduce -ag pattern

Materials / In-Class Assignments	Homework Assignments
Mon. Making Words manipulatives	Mon. Word building at home.
Tues. All About Magnets (Krensky; Scholastic; 1992)	Tues. Practice spelling test
Wed. Making Words manipulatives	Wed. Dragon art project–fill in dragon with -ag words
Thurs. Poem: Dragons, Dragons	Thurs. Practice spelling test
Fri. Test	Fri. Test

Evaluations: Spelling test

Pyramid	Notes
What some students will learn: challenge words: large, charge, dragon, magnet	1) Match Krista with a Making Words buddy (Tara) 2) Pull Krista, Thom, Justin, and Carlos for review on Thursday
What most students will learn: -ag pattern	
What all students should learn: review of -ar, -at patterns	Mon. Word Building Tues. Read Aloud Wed. Word Sorting Thurs. Choral Reading Fri. Spelling Test

Note. Developed by Ruth Rogge, Silver Ridge Elementary School, Broward County, FL.

reading challenges so that they can master the patterns. Lessons also include words that are based on the review and target word patterns, but they are more complex in that they contain beginning or ending blends. Most students are expected to learn the more complex words for the weekly spelling test. Finally, lessons include some challenge words (usually multisyllable words) or "outlaw" words (words that break typical patterns or rules). Some students will learn those words as bonus words for the spelling test. All students are exposed to all words in the lesson.

On Monday Ms. Wagner introduces the review and target words through a whole-class word-building exercise that takes about 30 minutes. She has found that even though the students used letter tile manipulatives during the lesson, some students need more support. Therefore, she has provided two of her students with a "*Making Words Buddy*"—another student who can provide support and encouragement during the lesson. She also sends home a list of words of the week to parents. (Spelling words for the weekly test consist of *Making Words* patterns, basic sight words, and key words from the basal reading series). On Tuesday Ms. Wagner introduces a trade book or a poem that incorporates the new word pattern for the week, and she reads the story aloud to students. On Wednesday she repeats the word-building activity and introduces a word-sorting activity to draw attention to features of each word pattern. On Thursday she has all students do a choral reading of the related book or poem. She also meets in a small group with four students who have challenges in learning to read and spell to provide additional practice. On Friday students are tested on the review and target words. Some students, based on their spelling needs, are graded only on the words at the base of the Pyramid; they are encouraged to *try* the words at the middle of the Pyramid and the bonus words at the top of the Pyramid.

Ms. Wagner has found that using the Pyramid for planning word recognition and spelling instruction has helped her tailor her teaching for individual student needs while teaching the class as a whole. Students with disabilities are less overwhelmed and frustrated because learning tasks are more manageable for them. Not only has she seen improvement of student spelling on weekly tests, but she has also noticed a transfer of what they have learned to their daily reading and writing activities.

What additional information is available?

Carson-Dellosa Publishing Co. (1994). *Introducing word families through literature*. Greensboro, NC: Author.

References

Adams, M. J., & Bruck, M. (1995). Resolving the "Great Debate." *American Educator, 19,* 7–20.

Cunningham, P. M., & Hall, D. (1994a). *Making big words: Multilevel, hands-on spelling and phonics activities.* Parsippany, NJ: Good Apple.

Cunningham, P. M., & Hall, D. (1994b). *Making words: Multilevel, hands-on developmentally appropriate spelling and phonics activities.* Parsippany, NJ: Good Apple.

Hall, D. P., & Cunningham, P. M. (1996). Becoming literate in first and second grades: Six years of multimethod, multilevel instruction. In D. J. Leu, C. K. Kinzer, & K. A. Hinchman (Eds.), *Literacies for the 21st century: Research and practice: Forty-fifth Yearbook of The National Reading Conference* (pp. 195–204), Chicago: The National Reading Conference.

Schumm, J. S., Vaughn, S., Haager, D., McDowell, J., Rothlein, L., & Saumell, L. (1995). General education teacher planning: What can students with learning disabilities expect? *Exceptional Children, 61,* 335–352.

Vaughn, S., Hughes, M. T., Schumm, J. S., & Klingner, J. (1998). A collaborative effort to enhance reading and writing instruction in inclusion classrooms. *Learning Disabilities Quarterly, 21,* 57–74.

Adaptation 6: Planning Pyramid for Multilevel Mathematics Instruction

Many elementary students with learning disabilities experience difficulties in basic mathematics computation skills and/or in problem solving (Peters et al., 1987). These difficulties frequently inhibit full participation in classroom mathematics instruction. Some intensive, direct instruction of students with special needs in learning mathematics (either individually or in small groups) may be necessary. However, with close attention to the scope and sequence of instructional content, to teaching strategies (e.g., Howell & Barnhart, 1992; Montague, 1992), and to the design of practice activities (e.g., Carnine, 1989) the level of participation and success of students can be greatly enhanced.

What is the adaptation?

The Pyramid provides an excellent framework for mathematics instruction. Many teachers have told us that most of their mathematics instruction is whole class. Students with learning disabilities as well as other students with challenges in learning computational and problem-solving skills were frequently lost and trapped in a downward spiral. The Pyramid can help teachers think about attending to differentiated student needs while thinking about the needs of the class as a whole.

In using the Planning Pyramid for mathematics instruction, the following questions need to be considered:

1. What is the skill or concept to be taught?

2. What are the prerequisites for this skill or concept?

3. What does it take for students to master this skill or concept?

4. What are extensions and applications of the skill or concept?

What does it look like in practice?

Mr. Miller teaches third grade students in a large, urban elementary school. He uses the Planning Pyramid for preparing for whole-class lessons in mathematics. As Mr. Miller puts it,

> With the right adaptations, I can get all my students to the top of the Pyramid! I still work with small groups of students to help them develop their computational skills. Some of my students have not become automatic in using basic facts or in basic operations; they need extra help. But they also like to feel part of the class; I don't want to separate them too much. That's why I use the Planning Pyramid—it makes me think about adaptations and how they can provide support for students who need that little boost.

Mr. Miller used the Planning Pyramid to develop a unit on money (see Figure 6). He used manipulatives, calculators, and cooperative learning groups to provide support for students who needed it. For two students, he needed to provide an oral, rather than a written, examination. As Mr. Miller told us, "All in all, planning for individual differences doesn't take much more time. It's worth the effort when I see students succeeding and feeling part of what we're doing in class."

What additional information is available?

Cuevas, G., & Driscol, M. (Eds.). (1993). *Reaching all students with mathematics.* Reston, VA: National Council of Teachers of Mathematics.

FIGURE 6
Unit Plan—Money

Unit Title: Money

Grade: 2

What SOME students will learn:
- Write and solve money word problems.
- Give correct change (act out and on paper).
- Given a certain amount of money, pick two things that are affordable.

What MOST students will learn:
- Add and subtract using pennies, dimes, and nickels.
- Using price tags, pay for items with coins.
- Read and write different money values.
- Match coins with certain prices.
- Show money equivalents between dimes, nickels, pennies, and quarters.

What ALL students will learn:
- Use terms *penny, nickel, dime, quarter, cost, price, buy, sell,* and *money.*
- Act out the process of "buying" and "selling" goods.
- Recognize and name the penny, nickel, dime, and quarter.
- Recognize the cent symbol.
- Read price tags.

Equipment/Supplies:
- Plastic money for manipulation.
- Price tags.
- Items to buy and sell.
- Real coins for identification.
- Create a store in the classroom.

Activities/Adaptations:
- Play store.
- Combine a hands-on manipulative approach with an audio/visual approach to create an atmosphere where all students can learn.
- Create a learning center with price tags for independent learning.
- Use homogeneous and heterogeneous cooperative learning groups to enhance learning for everyone.
- Use peer tutoring for help with manipulations.

Assessment:
- Observational rubrics.
- Problems of the day.
- A final test.

Lambie, R. A., & Hutchens, P. W. (1986). Adapting elementary school mathematics instruction. *TEACHING Exceptional Children, 18*(3), 185–189.

Vaughn, S., Bos, C. S., & Schumm, J. S. (1999). *Teaching exceptional, diverse, and at-risk students in the general education classroom* (2nd ed). Boston: Allyn & Bacon.

References

Carnine, D. (1989). Designing practice activities. *Journal of Learning Disabilities, 22*, 603–607.

Howell, S. C., & Barnhart, R. S. (1992). Teaching word problem solving at the primary level. *TEACHING Exceptional Children, 24*(2), 44–46.

Montague, M. (1992). The effects of cognitive and metacognitive strategy instruction on the mathematical problem solving of middle school students with learning disabilities. *Journal of Learning Disabilities, 25*, 230–248.

Peters, E., Lloyd, J., Hasselbring, T., Goin, L., Bransford, J., & Stein, M. (1987). Effective mathematics instruction. *TEACHING Exceptional Children, 19*(2), 30–33.

3. Simplifying or Supplementing Existing Materials

One goal of the Planning Pyramid is to provide all students with access to the curriculum. Teachers, researchers, parents, and even students frequently express concern that students with disabilities have limited exposure to the general education curriculum or that the curriculum is minimized to the point that students are inhibited in their opportunity to learn. At the elementary school level, students with special learning needs frequently can become full participants in regular classroom instruction with adaptations made by simplifying or supplementing existing materials. The goal is not to reduce content, but to provide tools for students to access content in the fullest sense. Simplification of existing materials can take many forms:

- Rewriting instructional materials in a simplified format.

- Providing summaries, graphic organizers, or outlines of instructional materials.

- Developing study guides to provide support before, during, and after reading.

- Reducing the length of reading or math assignments.

- Adjusting the pacing of assignments to allow for rereadings.

- Color-coding textbooks to highlight key concepts and new vocabulary.

- Audiotaping textbook content.

Supplementing existing materials involves the use of alternative materials to help students master the same content or skills presented in the general curricular materials. Such adaptations include using

- Direct experiences.

- Films or videotapes.

- Computer software.

Simplifying or supplementing existing materials can be time consuming for teachers. They try to make all of the adaptations themselves at the last minute and are not satisfied by the product. Teachers who plan for such adaptations in advance frequently engage parent volunteers or paraprofessionals in adapting materials.

When done in an organized manner, providing instructional "training wheels" for students is worth the effort. Students of all achievement groupings appreciate teachers who make adaptations for students who need them, and most students prefer using materials that are identical to those used by their same-age peers (Vaughn, Schumm, Niarhos, & Daugherty, 1993). Advance planning can help a teacher create materials that will make these types of adaptations routine and provide a bank of resources to draw upon for future classes. Volume 3 of this series provides concrete suggestions for implementation of such adaptations. Adaptations described in this section are

- Story Reading Guides.

- Audiotaping.

Adaptation 7: Story Reading Guides

Story reading can and should be enjoyable for elementary school students. Unfortunately, even when students' decoding is adequate, story reading assignments are troublesome for some young readers. Some children have difficulty with the cognitive task of remembering and retrieving story details and key story components. Others are unfamiliar with basic story structure due to lack of exposure to literature. Still other youngsters are familiar with alternative story structures due to cultural differences or are more comfortable with oral storytelling traditions than with sharing stories through print.

One way to provide students with a "blueprint for learning" from narrative text is a story reading guide. Story reading guides are a way to structure reading and learning from stories to enhance students' comprehension and their ultimate appreciation of the author's words. They are a way to simplify story reading assignments.

What is the adaptation?

Story reading guides can take a number of forms. Idol and Croll (1987) and Zipprich (1995) have suggested the use of story maps or webs—graphic organizers that students complete as they read a story. Components of a story map include setting and key elements of the plot. For primary grade students and other early readers, Smith and Bean (1983) suggested the use of picture representations. After listening to or reading a story, students illustrate key story features in cartoon-like form.

The Guide for Story Reading (Figure 7) not only provides students with a way to record key story components while reading, it also provides a strategy guide for before and after reading. The Guide for Story Reading consists of five steps:

1. *Get Ready.* Activities before reading that help students get involved in the story, activate prior knowledge about the story's setting and focus, and predict what the story will be about.

2. *Get Set.* A set of activities to complete after reading the first few pages of the story.

3. *Go.* Activities during reading that prompt active reading.

4. *Cool Down.* Activities to complete immediately after reading the story that promote immediate recall and help students record information to review for tests or classroom discussion.

5. *Follow Up.* Activities to promote critical thinking about the story or to promote appreciation. Follow-up activities can include art, writing, drama, cooking, or additional reading activities.

What research backs it up?

Research in explicit instruction in story elements indicates that such instruction can help students identify most relevant information (Idol

---

FIGURE 7
Guide for Story Reading

STEP 1: GET READY

- Read the title page.
- Skim through the book, looking at illustrations.
- Answer these questions:

What is the title of the story? _____

Who is the author of the story? _____

Who is the illustrator of the story? _____

What is the setting of the story? _____

   Time in history _____

   Place _____

What do I predict this story will be about? _____

_____

STEP 2: GET SET

- Read the first few pages or first chapter.
- Identify the main characters in the story.
- Answer these questions:

Who are the main characters in the story? _____

_____

Do the characters remind me of anyone I know? _____

_____

STEP 3: GO

- Read the rest of the story.
- Stop from time to time while reading to summarize what is going on in the story and to react to the story.
- Revise any of the information that you have already recorded above.
- Answer these questions:

What are the key events in the story? _____

_____

_____

What were the major problems that the character(s) had? _____

_____

How did they solve their problems? _____

_____

continues

47

FIGURE 7 *(Continued)*

STEP 4: COOL DOWN
- Think about what you read.
- Answer these questions:

What was the part of the story you liked best? _____

_____

What was the part of the story you liked least? _____

_____

Would you recommend this story to a friend? Why or why not? _____

_____

STEP 5: FOLLOW UP
- Think about a follow-up for this book. Write down our next activity.

_____

_____

& Croll, 1987), better understand story structure (Beck & McKeown, 1981), and improve students' story writing (Gambrell & Chasen, 1991). Furthermore, self-questioning during reading can improve story comprehension (Carnine & Kinder, 1985).

What does it look like in practice?

Marilyn Eaton started the school year with a plan for teaching her third graders a way to read and appreciate as well as to write stories. She realized from previous years' experience that many of her students found this task to be daunting and that she needed to provide support for them in simplifying an overwhelming task. Her plan included the use of a Guide for Story Reading.

At the beginning of the year, Marilyn used the Guide for Story Reading as a whole-class activity related to stories she read aloud in class. She used teacher modeling and guided instruction to help students become familiar with the five steps. Marilyn said, "I'm happy that I started this as a listening activity. I selected stories that I knew they would find interesting. We were able, then, to focus on the steps of the Guide for Story Reading and really get a handle on the sequence."

Marilyn then decided to pull a group of five students to demonstrate how to use the Guide for Story Reading as a cooperative learning activity. The students read a short story aloud to each other and worked together before, during, and after reading to complete the guide. The group presented the process to the whole class in a "fish bowl" demonstration—the group sitting in the middle of the classroom with other students all around.

As the school year progressed, Marilyn continued using the cooperative learning activity once a week to help students read basal reader stories or short trade books. She also had students use the question prompts in the guide for students to plan their own narrative writing. As she observed students in the cooperative learning groups, she noted that a few students with reading and learning disabilities needed additional support. Consequently, she pulled a small group of students for a teacher-led series of lessons to provide additional instruction in using the guide.

Marilyn evaluated the Guide for Story Reading as follows:

> Toward the end of the year I really began seeing results. Not only have students improved in their story reading skills, the quality of their story writing has improved as well. The guide was a tool I initially wanted to use to simplify the task of story reading and writing for students with special needs. What I discovered is that all students have benefited. The cooperative learning groups were extremely helpful for providing students with extra support and practice. The groups got really creative in working together to create follow-up activities.

What additional information is available?

Boyle, J. R., & Yeager, N. (1997). Blueprints for learning: Using cognitive frameworks for understanding. *TEACHING Exceptional Children, 29*(4), 26–31.

Hagood, B. F. (1997). Reading and writing with help from story grammar. *TEACHING Exceptional Children, 29*(4), 10–14.

Montague, M., & Graves, A. (1993). Improving students' story writing. *TEACHING Exceptional Children, 25*(4), 36–37.

References

Beck, I., & McKeown, M. G. (1981). Developing questions that promote comprehension: The story map. *Language Arts, 58,* 913–918.

Carnine, D., & Kinder, D. (1985). Teaching low-performance students to apply generative and schema strategies to narrative and expository material. *Remedial and Special Education, 6,* 20–30.

Gambrell, L. B., & Chasen, S. P. (1991). Explicit story structure instruction and the narrative writing of fourth- and sixth-grade below-average readers. Reading Research and Instruction, 31, 54–62.

Idol, L., & Croll, V. J. (1987). Story-mapping training as a means of improving reading comprehension. *Learning Disabilities Quarterly, 10,* 214–229.

Smith, M., & Bean, T. W. (1983). Four strategies that develop children's story comprehension. *Reading Teacher, 37,* 295–301.

Vaughn, S., Schumm, J. S., Niarhos, F., & Daugherty, T. (1993). What do students think when teachers make adaptations? *Teaching and Teacher Education, 9,* 107–118.

Zipprich, M. (1995). Teaching web-making as a guided planning tool to improve student narrative writing. *Remedial and Special Education, 16,* 3–15.

Adaptation 8: Audiotaping

One of the questions most frequently posed by classroom teachers for second grade and up is, "What can I do to keep a child in other subject areas if he or she just can't decode or write?" Study guides will not work. One-to-one instruction with a trained professional is not feasible. The most frequent answer to this most frequent question is: Use audiotapes.

Intuitively, audiotaping makes sense. If the teacher cannot be there physically to read aloud to a student, audiotaping offers an alternative. Audiotaping provides students with access to information so that they can continue to learn vocabulary and concepts. Audiotapes of commonly used textbooks are available from the nonprofit organization Recordings for the Blind and Dyslexic for students with visual impairments as well as students with learning disabilities. Fiction books are available from Talking Books, and most public libraries carry book-and-tape sets. Moreover, commercial audiotaped books are more accessible than in the past and are more socially acceptable in the eyes of the general public. If particular books are not available, teachers, parents, volunteers, and other students can read assignments into a tape recorder that the student with reading difficulties can listen to.

What is the adaptation?

Audiotapes can be verbatim tapes that students can use to read along with a textbook or trade book. In this way they can be an alternative way to present assignments for students who have basic reading skills. An audiotape can also be used as a substitute for a textbook. If a student cannot read a text at all, the student can listen to the audiotape instead of reading.

As Schumaker, Deshler, and Denton point out in Volume 3 of this series, if students listen to a tape in a passive manner, little learning is likely to occur. Strategies such as S.O.S.[4] provide students with a system for active listening to audiotapes through self-questioning.

The following are some basic dos and don'ts for effective use of audiotapes as an instructional adaptation:

DO

- Contact Recordings for the Blind and Dyslexic or Talking Books considerably in advance of the lesson to order what students may need.

- Enlist the help of students, volunteers, and/or paraprofessionals in recording audiotapes that are not otherwise available.

- Provide guidelines for individuals who make recordings, such as (a) speak in a natural voice and (b) speak at a pace that is considerate to the listener.

- Begin each tape by stating the title of the book or chapter, the author, and the page number at which the side starts. Provide a consistent system as you develop your library of tapes.

- Provide students with a simple listening guide—particularly if the textbook is too difficult for the student to follow along.

- Use audiotapes to record key ideas from mathematics books, particularly math word problems and directions for completing math assignments.

- Construct some audiotapes that are paraphrases of the textbook or that pull out key ideas from the text—particularly if recording or listening time is limited.

---

[4]S.O.S: Survey, Obtain Information, Self-test. This adaptation can be found in Volume 3 of this series, *Adapting Language Arts, Social Studies, and Science Materials for the Inclusive Classroom*, pp. 34–36.

- Prerecord tests that students are unable to read so that they are not dependent on the teacher and the teacher can attend to all students' needs during test taking.

- Allow *all* students access to audiotaped materials for some parts of their instruction, including gifted and talented students who may have advanced assignments (e.g., they can compare an author's reading of a text to their own interpretation).

DON'T

- Place students who cannot read in an embarrassing situation in the use of audio equipment. Find a quiet place, enlist the help of the special education teacher or parent, or provide a listening buddy. Students will not want to use audiotapes if there is a negative stigma associated with the process.

- Use audiotapes as a substitute for intensive reading instruction.

Audiotapes should be thought of as a temporary tool to convey information, not as a permanent substitute for learning to read.

What does it look like in practice?

Michael Voss is a fifth grade general education teacher. Miguel, a student with learning disabilities, is included in his classroom during math class. Miguel's calculation and problem-solving skills are on or above grade level. However, he cannot read well enough to read the mathematics textbook or math problems. At a conference at the beginning of the school year, Miguel's mother and father explained that they wanted to help Miguel, but that their own knowledge of math concepts was dated at best, and they were afraid that they would only confuse him if they tried to help at home.

Michael enlisted the help of a retired math teacher, Sam Young, to make audiotapes for Miguel. The volunteer paraphrased or read verbatim key concepts in the textbook. Sam also inserted questions along the way to help Miguel think about new ideas being presented. Sam read all directions for practice exercises—always inserting page numbers so Miguel could follow along. He also recorded all word problems so that Miguel could complete all homework assignments. Making the audiotapes was time consuming but worthwhile. Miguel's parents were appreciative of the tapes and scheduled regular homework time for him to use the tapes to complete assigned work.

Who can provide additional information?

Recordings for the Blind
and Dyslexic
20 Roszel Road
Princeton, NJ 08540
1-800-221-4792

Talking Books
National Library Service
for Blind and Physically
Handicapped
Library of Congress
1291 Taylor Street, NW
Washington, DC 20542
202/707-5100

What additional information is available?

Hammeken, P. A. (1995). *Inclusion: 450 strategies for success.* Minnetonka, MN: Peytral.

Meese, R. L. (1992). Adapting textbooks for children with learning disabilities in mainstreamed classes. *TEACHING Exceptional Children,* 24(3), 49–51.

4. Teaching Strategies for Using Materials

One of the ultimate goals of teaching is to help students become independent learners. Learners who are knowledgeable about a variety of strategies for learning and who are aware of how and when to use those strategies are on their way to becoming successful learners on their own. Some children are strategic learners by nature; others can become strategic with a few hints and prompts. However, many students need adaptive instruction and additional support to make the strategies part of their ongoing learning repertoire.

Adaptations in this section include

- Collaborative Strategic Reading.

- SIR RIGHT: A Strategy for Math Problem Solving.

Adaptation 9: Collaborative Strategic Reading

College professors complain that freshmen students do not know how to read and learn from textbooks—and they blame high school teachers. High school teachers complain that students do not know how to read and learn from textbooks—and they blame middle school teachers. Middle school teachers blame elementary school teachers, teachers blame either students or parents, and so it goes.

Most elementary and middle school reading curricula at least mention strategies for reading expository (informational) text. Frequently, however, students are not provided with enough supervised practice to make the strategies part of their ongoing repertoire of reading and study practices. Simply being "aware" of a strategy is not enough— particularly for students with reading and learning disabilities. What is needed is systematic and intensive practice in applying strategies to content area text with lots of support from both teachers and peers. The cycle of blame will end only when students truly are provided with opportunities to become independent, strategic learners early on.

What is the adaptation?

Collaborative strategic reading (CSR) combines both reading comprehension strategy instruction to provide students with systematic ways to read and learn from text and collaborative learning to provide students with the support they need from peers. It is most appropriate for students in grades three and higher. Some third grade teachers have reported that they first introduce CSR in third grade in small groups as part of a teacher-led center activity and later work toward cooperative learning groups. In addition, teachers in lower grades have introduced the language of CSR in whole-class reading activities.

The CSR routine actually includes four strategies that many elementary school teachers already incorporate in their reading curriculum: preview (generating prior knowledge and prediction about the topic), "click and clunk" (clarifying difficult vocabulary), get the gist (determining the main idea of units of text), and wrap up (summarizing the key ideas of the assigned passage and predicting questions that might be on a test). Each strategy is introduced one at a time to the whole class through teacher and student modeling. Students then implement the strategies in their cooperative learning groups.

The cooperative learning groups consist of four or five students. Each student is assigned a role and keeps that role for several weeks. Roles can include leader (guides fellow students through the strategies), clunk expert (leads discussion about how to "fix up clunks," confusion about difficult vocabulary), time keeper, recorder, and encourager. The cooperative learning groups ensure that all students have an opportunity to participate and be truly active learners.

During CSR sessions the teacher's role is to introduce the topic (including particularly difficult technical vocabulary students are likely to encounter), facilitate and monitor cooperative learning among small groups, and summarize key points at the end of the lesson.

Teachers frequently balance CSR sessions with other content area learning activities such as projects, experiments, and other hands-on activities. CSR sessions might be held twice a week (for approximately 1 hour), with other activities and tests being scheduled on remaining days.

What research backs it up?

CSR has been investigated in isolation (Klingner, Vaughn, & Schumm, 1998) and as part of a comprehensive reading plan (Vaughn, Hughes, Schumm, & Klingner, 1998) in general education classrooms that include students with disabilities and students who are English-language learners. It has also been investigated in special education settings with students who use English as a second language (Klingner & Vaughn, 1996). These investigations have yielded encouraging findings about the impact of CSR on the reading comprehension, vocabulary acquisition, and mastery of content area information on teacher-made tests. Teachers have taught us that CSR is more difficult to get up and running than some other instructional practices because it involves multiple strategies and cooperative learning. Nevertheless, persistence pays off. When CSR is used on an ongoing basis students become more strategic learners and learn how to study together in productive ways.

What does it look like in practice?

Mrs. Burt uses CSR for science instruction twice a week (Tuesdays and Thursdays). Mondays and Wednesdays are days for experiments. Fridays are for whole-class review or tests.

Mrs. Burt realizes that the purpose of CSR is slow and careful reading. It takes time. Therefore, she selects passages from the science textbook that focus on key ideas and that she really wants students to learn for a test. It would be impossible to read the entire chapter during CSR lessons, so Mrs. Burt also provides a study guide for students to use for reading the chapter as a whole.

Mrs. Burt begins each CSR lesson by introducing the topic for the day and teaching two or three technical vocabulary words that she knows are probably unfamiliar to most students and that they will need to learn. Students then preview the entire assignment for the day in their cooperative learning groups, thinking about what they already know about the topic and what they can predict they will learn. Students then read the assigned passage one paragraph at a time. After each paragraph they clarify unfamiliar terms (click and clunk) and work together to decide on the main idea of the paragraph (get the gist). The group's time keeper moves the group along and helps to keep students on task. Mrs. Burt circulates around the room to help clarify misconceptions, teach when needed, and ensure that all students are actively involved. Toward the end of the lesson students work in their groups to complete a wrap-up—determining the main ideas and concepts they learned and what questions are likely to be on a test. Mrs. Burt concludes the lesson with a whole-class discussion about key ideas and questions.

Mrs. Burt has this to say about CSR:

> What I like most about CSR is that my students with reading and learning disabilities have learned to take risks. They have learned that "clunks" are OK—that it is OK to ask questions and get clarification about what is new or unfamiliar. Best of all, CSR is helping all my students become more strategic readers. I used to teach SQ3R[5] once or twice a year, and students never caught on. I have learned that students of all achievement levels need regular practice with strategies if they are ever really going to learn to use them on their own.

What additional information is available?

Johnson, D. W., & Johnson, R. T. (1989). Cooperative learning: What special educators need to know. *The Pointer, 33*(2), 5–10.

Klingner, J. K., & Vaughn, S. (1998). Using collaborative strategic reading. *TEACHING Exceptional Children, 30*(6), 32–37.

References

Klingner, J. K., & Vaughn, S. (1996). Reciprocal teaching of reading comprehension strategies for students with learning disabilities who use English as a second language. *Elementary School Journal, 96,* 275–293.

Klingner, J. K., Vaughn, S., & Schumm, J. S. (1998). Collaborative strategic reading during social studies in heterogeneous fourth-grade classrooms. *Elementary School Journal, 99,* 3–22.

Robinson, F. P. (1970). *Effective reading* (4th ed.). New York: Harper & Row.

Vaughn, S., Hughes, M. T., Schumm, J. S., & Klingner, J. K. (1998). A collaborative effort to enhance reading and writing instruction in the inclusion classroom. *Learning Disabilities Quarterly, 21,* 57–74.

---

[5]SQ3R—The Survey, Question, Read, Recite, Review strategy (Robinson, 1970).

Adaptation 10: SIR RIGHT: A Strategy for Math Problem Solving

Students with learning disabilities may have difficulty with basic counting and computational skills in mathematics. Students with and without disabilities also have difficulties in solving math word problems. Indeed, math word problems are the Achilles heel of many students. (This was parodied in a *Far Side* cartoon that pictured Hell's library stocked only with books consisting of math word problems.) The fact is that word problems are designed to show real-world applications of mathematics. Their primary purpose (although it escapes many a student) is to make mathematics genuinely come alive.

Solving word problems is a complex cognitive task. Think about what is going on: Reading and mathematics are merged; words are sometimes used instead of numbers (e.g., *dozen*); the necessary mathematics operation is not explicitly called for; and sometimes multiple operations are necessary. On top of that, assuming that the correct operation(s) are selected, careful calculation is needed to derive the correct answer. No wonder word problems are overwhelming for elementary students! The complexity of solving word problems necessitates strategic thinking. The dilemma is that many students with disabilities lack systematic strategies for tackling word problems (Peters et al., 1987).

What is the adaptation?

SIR RIGHT, developed by Radencich (in Radencich & Schumm, 1997), is a strategy to help students tackle word problems in a systematic and consistent way.[6] The strategy consists of eight steps that can help students become actively engaged in problem solving. The steps are as follows:

1. Start by reading the entire problem either aloud or silently. Do not start solving the problem until you get the big picture.

2. Identify and highlight or circle all numbers—including hidden numbers (i.e., numbers written as words). If you can't write in your textbook, write all numbers on a piece of scratch paper.

3. Read the problem again. This time, try to draw a picture of the problem.

---

[6]From *How to Help Your Child with Homework*, by Marguerite C. Radencich, Ph.D. and Jeanne Shay Schumm, Ph.D. © 1997. Used with permission from Free Spirit Publishing, Minneapolis, MN; 1-800-735-7323; www.freespirit.com; ALL RIGHTS RESERVED.

---

4. Read the problem once again. This time, think: What is the problem asking for? What should my final answer be? What form should my final answer take?

5. Inquire. Ask yourself: What operation do I need to use to find the answer (add, subtract, multiply, or divide)?

6. Guess, to get a general estimate of what the answer should be. Should I end up with a larger number or a smaller number?

7. Ham it up! Act out the problem if necessary. Try to make it real. Use manipulatives if necessary.

8. Take a pencil and calculate the answer. Double check your answer to make sure it makes sense.

What research backs it up?

While SIR RIGHT has not been investigated formally, it is based on previous research in reading and mathematics education. First, SIR RIGHT relies heavily on repeated readings to improve comprehension. Second, it includes key components of effective mathematics strategy instruction for students with learning difficulties: use of manipulatives, estimation, visualization, and self-checking (e.g., Cawley, Miller, & School, 1987; Montague, 1992).

What does it look like in practice?

The general and special education teachers in Aileen Burt's school decided to teach all students the same math word-problem-solving strategy. Many teachers taught different versions of word-problem-solving strategies—many with similar components. What they found, however, was that differences in sequence, language, and steps were getting students confused—particularly students who were not strategy learners to begin with.

The teachers decided on the SIR RIGHT strategy because they thought it would be easy for students to remember. They even identified a "knight in shining armor" logo to accompany bulletin boards and handouts associated with the strategy.

In her fourth grade general education class, Aileen designed SIR RIGHT strategy guides to help her students (see Figure 8). Overall, Aileen saw the progress students made in using the guide and discovered that they eventually internalized the process. However, even with consistent and regular use of the strategy in class, she found that some of her students with more pronounced reading and learning disabili-

FIGURE 8
SIR RIGHT Strategy Guide

Directions: Read through each step of the SIR RIGHT strategy. After you complete each step, make a check in the box to show that you have completed the step.

Start by reading the whole problem. Don't starting solving the problem until you've read the WHOLE THING.
- ☐ I read the WHOLE problem.

Identify all numbers, including hidden numbers.
- ☐ I found all numbers, including hidden numbers.
- ☐ I wrote all numbers on a scratch piece of paper.

Read the problem again. This time, draw a picture of the problem.
- ☐ I read the problem again.
- ☐ I drew a picture of the problem on a scratch piece of paper.

Read the problem again. This time, think, "What is the problem asking for?" "What should my final answer be?"
- ☐ I read the problem again.
- ☐ I decided what the problem was asking for.
- ☐ I decided what my final answer should be.

Inquire. Ask yourself, "What operation do I need to use?" "Do I need to use more than one operation?"
- ☐ I decided what operation or operations to use. I am going to:
    - ☐ Add
    - ☐ Subtract
    - ☐ Multiply
    - ☐ Divide

Guess, to get an estimate of what the answer should be. Think, "Should I end up with a larger number or a smaller number?"

Ham it up! Act out the problem if necessary. Try to make it real. Use manipulatives if necessary.
- ☐ I tried to act out the problem.
    - *or*
- ☐ I used manipulatives to help me think through the problem.

Take a pencil and calculate the answer.
- ☐ I calculated the answer.
- ☐ I double-checked my calculations.
- ☐ I thought about my answer to make sure it makes sense.

ties still needed more support. Aileen worked with small groups of children to provide additional adaptations such as the following:

- Reading problems aloud to students.

- Rewriting problems in simpler language.

- Color-coding or highlighting key information in problems.

- Supplying problem-solving sheets that provide a framework for plugging numbers into a calculation.

- Supplying manipulatives or a calculator to assist with computation.

What additional information is available?

Cuevas, G., & Driscol, M. (Eds.). (1993). *Reaching all students with mathematics*. Reston, VA: National Council of Teachers of Mathematics.

Howell, S. C., & Barnhart, R. S. (1992). Teaching word problem solving at the primary level. *TEACHING Exceptional Children, 24*(2), 44–46.

Lambie, R. A., & Hutchens, P. W. (1986). Adapting elementary school mathematics instruction. *TEACHING Exceptional Children, 18*(3), 185–189.

References

Cawley, J. F., Miller, J. H., & School, B. A. (1987). A brief inquiry of arithmetic word-problem-solving among learning disabled secondary students. *Learning Disabilities Focus, 2*, 87–93.

Montague, M. (1992). The effects of cognitive and metacognitive strategy instruction on the mathematical problem solving of middle school students with learning disabilities. *Journal of Learning Disabilities, 8*, 230–248.

Peters, E., Lloyd, J., Hasselbring, T., Goin, L., Bransford, J., & Stein, M. (1987). Effective mathematics instruction. *TEACHING Exceptional Children, 19*(2). 30–33.

Radencich, M. C., & Schumm, J. S. (1997). *How to help your child with homework*. Minneapolis, MN: Free Spirit.

A Final Word

The introduction stated that this book is meant to be a handbook—providing basic tools for organizing the classroom for adaptations—and a sampler of materials adaptations that have been used successfully in elementary school classrooms. The search for multilevel instructional practices that can meet the needs of all learners and for materials adaptations for students with exceptional needs in the general education classroom is still in its infancy. The need for research and development in this area is imperative. In particular, there is a need for research and development that involves all stakeholders: university researchers, teacher educators, classroom teachers in general and special education, parents, and students. This type of collaboration is warranted if the goal is to integrate into classroom routines instructional practices that promote learning for all students, are feasible for classroom teachers to implement, and engage every student.